C. K. WILLIAMS

ALL AT ONCE

C. K. Williams's books of poetry include *Flesh and Blood*, which won the National Book Critics Circle Award; *Repair*, which won the Pulitzer Prize in Poetry; and *The Singing*, winner of the National Book Award. Williams was awarded the Ruth Lilly Poetry Prize in 2005. He has written a critical study, *On Whitman*; a memoir, *Misgivings*; and two books of essays, the most recent of which is *In Time: Poets, Poems, and the Rest*. He is a member of the American Academy of Arts and Letters.

ALSO BY C. K. WILLIAMS

POETRY

A Day for Anne Frank / Lies / I Am the Bitter Name / The Lark. The Thrush. The Starling. (Poems from Issa) / With Ignorance / Tar / Flesh and Blood / Poems 1963–1983 / Helen / A Dream of Mind / Selected Poems / The Vigil / Repair / Love About Love / The Singing / Collected Poems / Creatures / Wait / Writers Writing Dying

ESSAYS

Poetry and Consciousness / On Whitman /
In Time: Poets, Poems, and the Rest

MEMOIR

Misgivings

TRANSLATIONS

Sophocles' Women of Trachis (with Gregory Dickerson) / *The Bacchae of Euripedes / Canvas*, by Adam Zagajewski (translated with Renata Gorczynski and Benjamin Ivry) / *Selected Poems of Francis Ponge* (with John Montague and Margaret Guiton)

CHILDREN'S BOOKS

How the Nobble Was Finally Found /
A Not Scary Story About Big Scary Things

ALL AT ONCE

C. K. WILLIAMS
ALL AT ONCE

FARRAR STRAUS GIROUX / NEW YORK

Farrar, Straus and Giroux

18 West 18th Street, New York 10011

Printed in the United States of America

Published in 2014 by Farrar, Straus and Giroux

First paperback edition, 2015

The Library of Congress has cataloged
the hardcover edition as follows:

Williams, C. K. (Charles Kenneth), 1936–
[Poems. Selections]
All at Once / C. K. Williams. — First edition.
pages cm
Includes bibliographical references.
ISBN 978-0-374-21642-9 (hardcover)
I. Title.

PS3573.I4483 A6 2014
811'.54—dc23

2013033024

Paperback ISBN: 978-0-374-53510-0

Designed by Quemadura

Farrar, Straus and Giroux books may be purchased for
educational, business, or promotional use. For information on
bulk purchases, please contact the Macmillan Corporate and
Premium Sales Department at 1-800-221-7945, extension
5442, or write to specialmarkets@macmillan.com.

www.fsgbooks.com
www.twitter.com/fsgbooks
www.facebook.com/fsgbooks

1 3 5 7 9 10 8 6 4 2

CATHERINE

ALWAYS

CONTENTS

I.

II. CATHERINE'S LAUGHTER

III.

I

THE LAST CIRCUS

The horse trainer's horse is a scrawny pony; its ribs show, and when it levers itself onto its battered pedestal, it looks more arthritic than I am. It's trained to nod its head "Yes," but you can tell it wouldn't care if what it's saying is "No," or "Never," or "Leave me alone, please."

His master also plays the clown—when he does, he looks like an accountant down on his luck: he's not very funny, we clap because we want him to be. He also juggles, though he keeps dropping the dumbbells and balls.

The girl who walks the tightrope, three feet off the ground, must be his daughter. Then she's the girl hanging from a long rope her clown-father swings; he lets her plummet down until her face nearly touches the sawdust, then she pops to her feet. Her costume is blotchy, and sags.

Intermission: behind the tent, the most bored lions in the world laze in their fetid cage, refusing to meet our eyes. Then a clutch of battered trailers, clotheslines slung from them out to some trees: T-shirts, towels, underclothes worn all but to air. Scattered beneath are crumpled pizza boxes, plastic bags, beer bottles, cans, other indecipherable junk.

The show begins again, the sparse audience climbs back onto the bleachers. One man sits engulfed by his children: a sleeping two-year-old sprawls across his lap, her head lolling on his shoulder; he kicks her gooey, half-eaten, half-melted glop of cotton candy into the void beneath; a larger child, another girl, sits on one of his knees, wriggling with delight, her circus banner waving in his face; and the last, a baby in the crook of his arm, he manages with the same hand that holds it to offer it some cola in a cup. A little dribbles on the baby's chin, and with a corner of his shirt he wipes it up, pats the disconsolate infant in his lap, who's just woken crying, and then, when the clown appears again, he cheers, stamps, whistles, and, like Shiva, foliates another pair of hands and heartily applauds.

SILENCE

The heron methodically pacing like an old-time librarian down the stream through the patch of woods at the end of the field, those great wings tucked in as neatly as clean sheets, is so intent on keeping her silence, extracting one leg, bending it like a paper clip, placing it back, then bending the other, the first again, that her concentration radiates out into the listening world, and everything obediently hushes, the ragged grasses that rise from the water, the light-sliced vault of sparkling aspens.

Then abruptly a flurry, a flapping, her lifting from the gravitied earth, her swoop out over the field, her banking and settling on a lightning-stricken oak, such a gangly, unwieldy contraption up there in the barkless branches, like a still Adam's-appled adolescent; then the cry, cranky, coarse, and wouldn't the waiting world laugh aloud if it could with glee?

MNEMOSYNE

As far as I know, I don't suffer from Alzheimer's or anything else so grim. I remember most of what I have to, and if occasionally someone's name skitters away from me, I've learned to announce without too much embarrassment that I'm having "a senior moment"—who came up with that so useful locution?—and I'm usually forgiven, or believe I am.

Sometimes in fact my memory can be too active, too frenetic, hopping about along unpredictable routes, dragging me sometimes to realms of blur in which I can barely make out old thoughts, old feelings, and even sometimes to places to which I feel a bit abashed to have taken myself. I remember for example with almost distressing clarity young women I long ago knew, and loved, or half loved, and, perhaps I should say, possessed, at least some of them. What a thick word: "possessed." I've never applied it to my life before, and I'll admit I feel more than a bit squeamish doing so: it feels like a term from another mode of being, so forceful, so definitive.

Anyway, there they are, these girls, these women, within me now, more specifically within that part of me . . . Wait, what part do I mean exactly? I reach for an analogy and come up with, inappropriately I hope, peep shows, those insidious, debasing chambers that exist, or existed, in emporiums for pornography . . . Or I'm told they did—I never had the inclination to slither into one of those surely disgusting, suffocating booths where males gaze out from their pathetic gloom at women simulating nakedness. Can't nakedness be simulated regardless of the condition of dress or undress of the object?

Yet it would seem here I am within my very own. I hope this isn't too despicable, what I'm doing, drawing my old sweethearts, my lust objects, my friends (once or twice), out of the peace and repose of time past, but there they are, so lifelike, their faces, their voices, their characters, their selves, their joy or delight or disappointment, even, touchingly, their bodies, which were one and all (this was, after all, decades ago) young, vibrant, unsullied by time's compromises.

Do I remember with delectation? Delight? I don't quite know. Perhaps the actual delight is in the ludicrously efficacious facility of memory. To remember those particular hips, those breasts, the suppleness of such and such a waist . . .

Sometimes it can feel that these entrapments of the past, derangements they might be, are a kind of sin. And how painful that the past can arrive so intensely, yet remain so cosmically elusive, so frozen in disjointed moments that even as I hold them before me, "possess" them, they dim, grow uncertain, become again mist.

As does, in truth, much else, for memory and its inconsistencies can be darker, more annihilating—there's so much I've forgotten, apparently irretrievably. Books, for one: the many novels the plots of which I've forgotten, the volumes of thought the central premises of which are so uncertain to me as to be all but useless, the poems I no longer can quote more than patches of. And music and movies and plays . . .

Occasionally, on a purely personal level, forgetting can be strange, bizarre—when I forget for instance about health problems I've had, when I can't remember within years when I had cancer, when my knees were replaced. And matters more trivial but as disorienting. Yesterday, when I was looking at the unusual insoles in a pair of shoes I was putting on, and tried to remember where they'd come from, why I had them at all, I couldn't. I could recall visiting a doctor a few years ago, and even the doctor, a pleasant woman about to have a baby, but not what had been wrong with me to bring me to her. After much flopping about in memory, I remembered I'd had pain in one of my feet, but not which foot, and not the name of what the doctor told me was the problem, nor how long it lasted, only that she'd suggested I use this insole, and it had helped me. Unsettling, not to remember the history of one's own body.

At the worst, it can feel my life is shrinking, if not quite physically then certainly as though the projectile my experiential self has always been is diminishing in density as it becomes longer in length, my dart through time more narrow, less forceful.

I recall there was a period after college when some of my artist friends and I—so young we were—mused longingly of "living in the moment," as the mystics and other enlightened souls we were studying were reputed to have done, but never did we dream what doing so might actually mean. The "moment" as we live it can be glorious, and full, and weigh and be savored, but there's much to be said too for the moment experienced again, savored again. How could we know back then that we were being tempted, as in one of those myths or folktales in which a protagonist isn't attentive enough to the implications of a wish about to be granted—Midas and his ilk?

I try not to think too much about this. My days are fine, I work, I don't work, I live, I love. I know if I am becoming senile, it's still benign, and not even terribly inconvenient. Any sadness comes down to having to realize I'm losing portions of the history I was innocently convinced I'd have with me to the end, while here the end is almost upon me, and where have those pieces of me gone?

THE BEGGAR

"If you don't want to give me money, or a job, or something to eat," he announces loudly to the subway car, "then why not adopt me? I'm cleaner than a dog, I'm housebroken, so I don't have to be walked." Most of us are amused, but still, not many come across with the handout he's really after. I don't, I just don't feel like it today, and besides I'm absorbed in a book, which seems excuse enough.

I look up, though, after he passes, and notice that a rather pretty girl down the aisle is smiling, and that when the beggar—he's surprisingly young, and surprisingly clean-cut, even good-looking—comes to her seat, he smiles back, and when she gets off at the next station he pops out too and strides beside her, chatting her up, she still smiling, obviously feeling not unfriendly towards him, or, more than that, leaving the rest of us, or me anyway, to wonder if the whole thing was a put-on, two kids on a lark, but no, he did look like he needed help, hair too oily, clothes stained past the cusp of respectability, neither of which seemed to bother the girl at all, so who knows, maybe we've had the chance to be present at the onset of an unlikely romance, something from a movie, a "cute meet" they call it, and can go back to what we'd been doing, our consciences, such as they are, absolved for once, at peace.

THE TWO VOICES OF

ELIZABETH BISHOP

On the same tape, the two voices: the younger, pert, perky, so early on already suffused with knowledge, it's tempting to say wisdom—though is knowledge wisdom? Then the later: a voice striated with the grittiness of time, of experience; the tone touched, just touched, by weariness, though with enough self-deprecation to indicate a really not overly debilitating weight of regret.

Young, imparting those blossomings of imagination the voice perhaps a little taken aback to have generated. Later, older: I did this, yes, it made some difference once, but I can't be bothered to remember what or when it would have been, though I still know it's there somewhere, and I still esteem it.

In neither voice is there any indication of the timbre being afflicted by tears, both as shriven of such matters as are their verse. There's only an echo of tears' deepest origins, the chamber beneath voice from which arise not only tears but everything else.

If there's early on a wide-eyed pride along with wonder at having accomplished what has been accomplished, in the later it's gone. Though there's still a tinge, a touch, a hint of satisfaction, perhaps brought about by the sheer inescapability of knowing what she's wrought, there's no residual narcissistic pride, except perhaps a tiny bit, layered deep within the jokey prosy preludes to the reading of the poems themselves.

Gone completely is the urgency of the younger, the barely suppressed rush, hurry, the need to bring forth, have brought forth, more, more. Enduring, the self-astonished patience that sanctioned it all.

NEITHER

Neither that I picked my nose compulsively, daydreamed through my boring classes, masturbated, once in a condom I stole from my father's drawer, enraptured by its half-chemical, half-organic odor; nor my obsessions with smells in general, earth, dead rats, even my baby sister's diaper shit, which made me pleasantly retch; nor that I filched money from my mother for candy and so knew early on I was a thief, a sneak, a liar: none of that convinced me I was "bad," subversive and perverse, so much as that purveyor of morality— parent, teacher, maybe even treacherous friend—who inculcated the unannulable conviction in me that the most egregious wrong, of which I was clearly already despicably, irredeemably guilty, was my abiding involvement with myself.

Even now, only rarely am I able to convince myself that my reluctance to pass on my most secret reflections, meditations, theorizings, all the modes by which I manage to distract myself, arises from my belief that out of my appalling inner universe nothing anyway could possibly be extracted, departicularized, and offered as an instance of anything at all to anyone else.

An overrefined sense of generosity, I opine; an unwillingness to presume upon others by hauling them into this barn, this sty, where mental vermin gobble, lust, excrete. Not a lack of sensitivity but a specialization of that lobe of it which most appreciates the unspoken wish of others: to stay free of that rank habitation within me I call "me."

Really, though: to consider one's splendid self-made self as after all benevolent, propelled by secret altruism? Aren't I, outer mouth and inner masticating self-excusing sublimations, still really back there in my neither-land?

Aren't I still a thief, stealing from some hoard of language trash to justify my inner stink?

Maybe let it go, just let it go.

DIVORCE

The first divorce in my parents' generation, when marriages rupturing was still something shameful, a perilous secret, like sex, was between the father and mother of a friend of mine. His family lived across the backyard from us in a two-story house; the upstairs was occupied by my friend's aunt and her husband and children.

We learned afterwards, or anyway I did, that my friend's parents had stayed together "for the children" for what must have seemed long years for both of them: their apartment was very small, there wasn't even enough room for an extra bed, so they'd have had to continue to share one.

The mother as I remember her was attractive, with dark hair, strong facial structure, and a nice build. The father—they're all dead now, even my friend, who died too young—was a printer, a "job printer," my father told me. He had a small shop, not far from my father's business, and wasn't partaking much in the postwar burst of prosperity that benefited so many others. What most intrigued me about him were three long, ragged scars he had across the back of his neck, dramatic, crisscrossing evidence of slashes he was reputed to have suffered in a fight with a black man, in what I once overheard someone aver was a wild youth.

His scars were even more exotic to me than the divorce would be later on. A violence was implied in them that seemed to go beyond mere self-defense: he had to have been in an environment where knives or, even more frightening, straight razors were common, and he had to have been close enough to his assailant and physically effective enough so that the scars came only partway around his neck. He'd have had to fight off his attacker face-to-face, not turn and run, because then he'd have had his throat cut, or so I fantasized it.

Physically, he was imposing—stocky, with a big, muscular gut, an invulnerable-seeming torso—a body it would be impossible to tip over. At home, though, he was gentle, taciturn, reserved, in a family in which everyone else, his wife and daughter and my friend, were, as my parents put it, "high-strung." I can hardly remember him uttering a word all the time I spent with my friend in their apartment. When his wife finally left him, he disappeared from our lives completely. I never heard anyone mention him again.

MORTALITY

The boy's grandmother keeps cutting the food on her plate into smaller and smaller pieces, and sometimes she cuts his food smaller, too, until his father tells her to stop. The boy worries, because not only is her food getting smaller, but her mouth is, and she is, and also she's more silent, and angrier to herself about things, her food, and matters she keeps to herself—he just can feel her getting angry in herself.

The way she's shrinking, he worries, soon maybe food won't fit in her at all, no matter how small she cuts it, no matter how exasperated with it she is.

One day, when he goes into the bathroom he shares with her and unzips, he sees a tiny, perfectly round poop she must have left in the toilet. As he pees, it rocks, sad and brown and bereft in the water at the bottom of the bowl.

So alone it looks, he wants almost to pop it into his mouth, to keep it, for her, for himself.

THE BROOM

The wide-bristled brooms that late at night in bus stations glide noiselessly over the terrazzo floors, as though they'd achieved the most intimate, unintimidated relation to duration, to time; as though, despite the tired salesman half asleep on a bench, the two college-kid lovers impatiently waiting in the dark sanctity of a Greyhound for the bus to depart so they can continue their furtive petting, the group of Asian women who huddle around a pay phone, listening, listening, waiting, hanging up then dialing again an instant later (what betrayal might they be involved in, what abandonment, desertion?), and the semi-winos and the semi-paranoid who are allowed to slump and sleep in these sanctuaries reserved for them, as well as we who are blessèd by the scriptures of our tickets—as though all of this might be systematically transcended, lifted from the precincts of a mere motorless implement patterning methodically over trivial shining expanses with a mad geometrical exactness, to a process more comprehensive, a tractor, say, in a wheat field after harvest, when every centimeter must be disked and harrowed, and all beneath a brutal August sun none of us trapped here has beheld for centuries, only fancied, dreamed of, here in this hallowed, middle place of bland fluorescent longing.

ART

Our high school art teacher, Miss Demarest, didn't really teach art, she didn't teach anything: she handed out supplies, paper and pencil, sometimes paint or colored chalk, sometimes if anyone was interested lumps of clay to fool around with, which I never did because all I wanted then was to draw horses.

Miss Demarest didn't care, though, what I or any of us drew. She'd just sit at her desk at the front of the art room, doing I have not the slightest notion what, and say hardly anything to us at all. We never realized this until one day we happened to have a substitute art teacher who actually put some pots on a table for us to sketch and came to our desks to make suggestions as to how we could improve our futile scribbles.

Then Miss Demarest was back, a little frumpy she was, not unpleasant, just utterly uninterested in us. But who knows? Maybe in secret she was a great artist who had to get through this onerous pedagogical obligation, just as Mozart had to with his students.

It's said Mozart loathed having to give lessons. I read somewhere that his procedure was to play through a piece on the piano, then tell his student, "Like that."

Well, at least afterwards you'd have the right to brag, "I studied with Mozart."

MANURE

A winter's worth of manure towering in the yard beside the stable. A winter's worth of stable warmth rising in the chilly early April air. I walk to the gate, lift the crude wire latch to let the still thick-furred foal into the meadow, then go through into the paddock. A breeze winds down through the stand of pines on the hill, a rooster releases its garbled call to the waking world.

This never happened to me, yet it's memory, too, thrashing in its pathetic confining containers of truth, avid to evoke pasts it was never privileged to possess, to elate itself with nostalgia for moments of other lives.

. . . In this case the boys I knew who lived in the country, the children of farmers, horse breeders, blacksmiths, and my friends whose father taught in the city but came back every night to their summer camp in rural New Jersey to his wife and two sons who'd grown up there.

I envied the sons their life in the country. I wasn't even jealous of how at home they were in the fields and woods and barns; of how they could do so many things I couldn't, drive tractors, take apart and fix motors, pluck eggs from under a hen, shove their way into a stall with a stubborn horse pushing back: I just marveled at it all, and wanted it. They and the boys who lived on farms near them were also so enviably at ease in their bodies: what back in the city would be taken as a slouch of disinterest, here was an expression of physical grace. No need to be tense when everything so readily submitted to your efficiently minimal gestures: hoisting bales of hay into a loft, priming a recalcitrant pump . . .

Something else there was as well, something more elusive: perhaps that they lived so much of the time in a world of wild, poignant odors—mown grass, the redolent pines, even the tang of manure and horse-piss-soaked hay. Just the thought of those sensory elations inflicted me with a feeling I still have to exert myself to repress that I was squandering my time, wasting what I knew already were irretrievable clutches of years, now hecatombs of years, trapped in my trivial, stifling life.

LAPHAM

In our junior year in high school, we were assigned to read *The Rise of Silas Lapham*. Although the title of the book (it's by William Dean Howells) refers to the rise of its protagonist, it's really more concerned with his fall: he's a businessman who makes some money, acquires a big house, then through no great fault or flaw of his own loses it all. As I recall, he's not a bad man, just naïve, innocent, a kind of American Ivan Ilyich. Also as I remember—I haven't reread the book since then—there's no redemptive ending, no epiphany or spiritual realization, just the recounting of how dreadful loss can be, of how oblivious we are to what lurks before us.

I've wondered sometimes whether the book with its dire message was inflicted on us with a specific purpose: somebody had to choose it, there were certainly better-written books available then. Perhaps, since so many families in the suburb where we lived were quite well-off and involved in material advancement, the teachers, or the board of education, thought it was a story we'd be able to attach to.

But given how harsh the plot was, they may possibly, consciously or not, have been trying to temper how self-satisfied we were, how oblivious to how we were sheltered from life's real risks. Maybe they were just trying to instill some humility in us, or might they simply have been irritated by us, or jealous—after all, in those days teachers were even more underpaid than now.

Either way, the book certainly made their point. The message that anything I might attain in my life will always to some degree be in jeopardy, at risk, that I might at any moment lose everything I have, insinuated into me, and stayed, nailed into my conscience like a floor.

THE SIGN PAINTER

The summer camp where I worked as a headwaiter when I was six-teen hired men off the Bowery in New York as its kitchen staff. When a position would come open, which was often because one of the men was always falling off the wagon and vanishing, one of the owners would go down to the city and come back with yet an-other derelict soul. Some of them lasted awhile; one, a chef, very gruff, standoffish, who never spoke to anyone when he didn't have to, kept going all summer.

Another, a slight, self-effacing middle-aged man, was hired as a dishwasher, but when the camp owners discovered he had once been a sign painter, they commissioned him to paint the camp logo on their station wagon in his spare time. I don't know whether he'd brought his brush and paints with him, or whether they'd bought them for him, but every day after lunch he'd be hunched on a stool with his slender brushes and the rod with a little ball on the end he used to steady his hand, painstakingly painting the logo—it was a hawk, I had no idea why—along with the name of the camp in ornate lettering.

I liked him and was bored by camp life, so I used to sit with him and watch him work, and I became something like his confidant, maybe because I paid attention to what he was doing, which no one else did. He worked remarkably carefully, slowly, I suspected too slowly: though he obviously knew his craft, I guessed that his almost obsessional meticulousness must have been an impediment to whatever chance he'd have had of doing this as a profession. Or perhaps it was the other way around: perhaps this had been his profession, and he'd left it because his life had collapsed, sent him to drink, then to the streets, and, wounded, he could only work this way now.

One afternoon, after I'd been watching him for a while, he started to tell me about his past. I don't remember all that much, but there was a period he'd spent working, or maybe it was just making bets, at racetracks, and he made it sound like the high point of his life. Whatever the details were, it didn't matter much to me—I realized he was offering me the sense of an existence of which I had absolutely no inkling: he was offering me his life itself, and I knew even then to be moved and grateful.

I've wondered why he'd chosen me: I was a naïve, sheltered adolescent, and all I can think of is that there must have been something about me that was so unthreatening that he was able to talk about himself in a way he certainly wouldn't have been able to with the kitchen drinkers with whom he had to spend most of his time. Their conversation, from what he told me, had almost entirely to do with binges past and present, and sexual adventures that may have been true but probably weren't.

I suppose I could have asked him to tell me more about what had brought him to where he was—if he'd ever had a family, or a real job, but I mostly just sat watching him work. He painted with a terrific focus, an intensity I'd never seen in an adult before—there was something heroic about it, and I suppose he was the first real artist I'd ever met.

One afternoon—he was about halfway finished with his painting—as I got up to go into the kitchen, he told me he'd be leaving soon. By then I understood what that meant, that he'd gone longer than he could without drinking, and though I'd learned to sympathize, I still felt a little betrayed, not so much for myself, but because he hadn't finished the task he'd undertaken. I knew the owners would be doubly irritated with him, first because they'd have to go find another dishwasher, but more because now the station wagon had a partly painted sign and there wasn't likely to be anyone in the rural area where the camp was to finish it, and that now they'd speak of him with contempt—they weren't at all nice people—and I'd feel humiliated for him.

The next day he was gone, and remarkably enough, I had a postcard from him a few weeks later from the racetrack at Saratoga: there were only a few words on it, but they were written in a calligraphy as striking as the one he'd been using on the station wagon. I kept it for a long time; it may have been the first thing in my life I treasured just for its own sake, without having to authenticate its worth by sharing it with someone else. I wish I still had it.

WIND

Last year in the region where we live part of the year there were violent windstorms, whole forests were leveled, two- and three-hundred-year-old trees torn up by the roots and tossed aside, houses sliced almost in half by the once-sheltering giants flung down through their roofs.

Yesterday another storm, powerful but less so, took down no trees. The ground, though, is littered with leaves, as though autumn had arrived, but the leaves are still green, still alive, many torn away in clumps, with the twigs still intact that attached them to their branches.

There's something disconsolate about them—the desiccated leaves of autumn always appear to have found the place to which they've been destined, but these don't seem to grasp what's happened to them: they lie on the ground at awkward angles, like things wounded that haven't completely given in to death and don't know yet they must.

MATH

Such pleasure to have lived in a reality in which numbers make their magically satisfying appearance. The teacher scribbles miracles on the blackboard, grown-up things vouchsafed to us, to *me*. I add, subtract, multiply, divide. Splendid how it happens in your life: second grade, long division; third grade, fractions, sixteen and two-thirds, five-fifths; then calculate a percentage: a little shuffle in the mind, a little blur that takes you, and clatter and click, the answer slides in like a bolt in a lock—oh, nothing else even comes close. Tangent, sine, and cosine, logarithms! Tens and tens, how they surge all by themselves into our lives, these secrets the cosmos ripened for us, these living webs reeled out to us that we cast back to make of reality line, graph, equation, all by which we conceive, reconceive, measure ourselves.

Sometimes, though, just sometimes, the sum, the total, the calculation is of stupidity, violence, suffering, arrogance. Pain and death—they add up, they multiply, too, they too partake: weapons, the dead, the number of poor, the number of starving, the number of souls wounded, souls maimed, betrayed, and hearts hardened beyond measure . . .

No, leave all that, better those archaic leaps to precision, algebra and calculus, numbers without bodies, numbers even imagined— square root of minus one, which I never wholly grasped because I played hooky that day—but never mind, what remains is this striving towards one truth, then two, then many, so many that even if I'll never comprehend them are still there, contemplating themselves, leaping with joy, in beauty, with infallible grace.

CHILD'S MIND

As I grow ever older, as I mature, I suppose would be the word, I become more and more aware of the parts of myself that don't arrive at anything like what might be implied by that grand term "maturity." I become more conscious instead of how trapped I am in a mind that in its perceptions, its impulses, its emotions, is very much a child's.

I've spent so much time, so much labor trying to tame this conceit we call mind, cajoling it to be more reasonable, more sensible, less stubborn, less simply silly. But the task is hopeless because my child's mind, the mind that lurks beneath all the other kinds of mental existence I like to think determine who I am, experiences the world in brute, crude, utterly unsophisticated systems of feeling and thought: it wants, it wishes, it desires—things, feelings, states of being—and when it isn't granted them to possess, or at least hope to possess, it becomes depressed or flies into a tantrum. And worse, it's not satisfied with half ways; it admits no partials, no gradations, no compromises or concessions: to it accommodations are capitulations, failures, precursors to defeat.

Further, that the world beyond me is not as my child's mind wishes it to be—imagines it can be, is passionately convinced it absolutely should be—throws it into a frenzy of frustration, exasperation, indignation, umbrage, so that I, trapped for so much of the time in this mind, am offended, embittered; I disapprove, I sulk, I become petulant. When I look out into reality, when I peer out between my petulance and sulk at that world which at once lacks and is in perilous danger—how can I not be fraught? How can my mind not be frightened not only of the world but also of itself, this juvenile consciousness that inflicts the imperfect world on itself?

But perhaps, if when I taught myself to complain that the world didn't work as it should, that so much so elementary was awry, when I came to fret that I'd been presented with a perfectible world, you just had to think hard about it, but I had thought about it, hard, and every day, and nothing had changed . . .

Perhaps, if when I'd begun bemoaning the fallible world, the unjust world, the world all but knocked from its axle by evil and indifference, if someone had told me, proved to me that I really had no idea how the world worked, that I'd been bemoaning all this time that the world should do something about itself, when what I actually wanted to change was how I was in it, how I devoured and digested it . . .

Perhaps if I'd been told, if I'd been taken by the shoulders and shaken and told, might I perhaps at last have understood?

SCENTS

Sweet to remember the tiny elevator I used to take to the garret someone had loaned me as an office and the way three people would crowd into its one-meter square and share our scents and stinks and emanations, even the half-thug from the floor below whose rock radio stations raged up through the ceiling at me but who must have spent half his pay on whatever cologne he soaked himself in, so raptly buoying it was.

And the woman who perfumed herself with something that threw me centuries back to some lost time of life I never lived but would passionately have liked to, and whom I suspect suspected by the way I inhaled her perfumes and powders and flesh scents, trying to keep them, keep them, that I was a clod and so manifested an edge of contempt in her glance at this pervert she was forced to slip past to get off.

And descending at lunchtime our rattling conveyance as patient as a donkey with two men from some Middle East country whose language I couldn't even name, how the rich reek of the meal they'd just eaten—onions and lamb—infused the minuscule volume of our shared air.

And once, outside on the sidewalk, a girl kissing her boyfriend goodbye, twice, thrice, who, as she swung before me, lifted the mass of her hair from her neck as though the day were terribly hot, which it wasn't at all, and I fancied the bouquets from that smooth nape trailing behind her like the cloud puffs from a skywriting airplane, so clear to me I felt if I walked a little higher on my toes, I could plunge my face in them and become a scented cloud myself.

KAHN

Reading a late book by one of my masters, Czeslaw Milosz, I come across a poem about a painting, with an epigraph indicating that it hangs in an art museum that was designed by another of my masters, the architect Louis Kahn. It pleases me to think of Czeslaw making his way through those serenely elegant, luminous spaces Lou had devised: Milosz hushed in the inspiration of his experience of it, the other embodied in the very hush.

From Milosz I wanted to learn, tried to learn, scale, scope, largeness of attention and attempt. From Lou, whom I knew when I was much younger, just starting out, I learned discipline and, most crucially, patience, which for him were the same thing: he never gave up on a project, no matter how long it took, until it had been brought to a level he would accept. I was awed by the way he would sit quietly sketching in his unpretentious office, and was intimidated by his fame, which was just then coming to him, late, but not too late.

I think he must have found me amusing—I was the only one in his social circle who ever disagreed with him or asked him to explain his sometimes garbled theoretical pronouncements. Most of those around him were the young architects who worked in his office, or students—protégés, acolytes—and they held him in such reverence that they unanimously nodded in agreement with everything he said, and some seemed to be frankly stricken in his presence, though he was a warm, sometimes funny, very accessible and likable man.

That meticulous patience brought him famously magnificent buildings, but much worldly frustration. He died bankrupt, mostly because of all the hours he and his associates put into his designs and all the revisions and recastings he'd demand before he'd allow a building to be built. He also lost many commissions, so many that a book, *Louis I. Kahn: Unbuilt Masterworks*, was recently published, in which there are computer-generated models of those structures that for one reason or another—usually foolishly impatient clients—exist only as drawings and models.

The structures in the computer images in the book are heartbreaking in their splendor, and also mysterious and evocative in a way actual buildings never are, and probably can't be. The originals were conceived of as stone, or poured concrete; the projections incorporate images with those materials, and the results have a moving solidity to them with no trivializing details such as furniture or people: never have buildings been so empty of footsteps, voices, the warmth of living bodies. It's saddening to realize that no one will ever walk through these luminous spaces, never exult in their volume and light as Milosz did in that celebrated museum in Texas.

Lou died before I ever had the chance to thank him for how he'd inspired me and how much he taught me. One of my favorite memories is of when I had what I thought was a brilliant design idea, which one day when I was hanging out at his office I presented to him. What if, I asked him, the interior elements of a building—

closets, dressers, bookshelves, even bathrooms—were expressed on the *outside*, so the inner life of the structure would be manifest in its exterior form?

There's actually a recent building in Paris—another museum— that does just this: some of its exhibition rooms protrude from the sides of the main structure. I have no notion if this "works" archi- tecturally or not, but anyway, when I offered my thought to Lou, he just smiled.

"Charlie," he said, "for a poet you're being awfully literal."

We both laughed, but I was moved. I'd announced long before that I wanted to be a poet, but I hadn't done anything, written any- thing to indicate I was or ever would really be one. I seemed always to be just starting, still waiting to begin, I was that far from any real accomplishment in my craft, from doing anything but struggling with my ineptitude. So to have Kahn refer to me as a poet, even jok- ingly ... What a gift that was then, what a precious memory now.

I KEPT CHANGING MY MIND

I kept changing my mind, not about the essentials, love, food, a warm bed, a life to live without anyone overtly intruding onto the already difficult endeavor of creating that problematic, a soul.

I kept changing my mind and clearing my throat and trying out tones of voice and methods of address (I also changed my mode of address as much as I could without appearing entirely and untrustworthily erratic) and the pitch and the syntax that would come rising in a clarity as twisted and touching as a tree's; also perhaps I changed along with everyone else in wondering whether it was a concept like freedom or a concrete like bread or some conceit more than mere bread that would include word, poem, book, which drove us so furiously that we didn't believe our own calm reasonings about the death that surely hungered for us and the infinite sleep that desired us, both of them ravenous for the best of us, the parts we knew best.

I kept changing my mind, suspecting all along that I'd be accused of vacillation and weakheartedness, and so accusing myself of vacillation and weakheartedness and of indolence, which Kafka said was impatience, but I could never bring myself to believe him, impatience being perhaps the only virtue I believed in, and I wasn't accustomed to accusing myself of virtues, only of what I needed to go on with this uncertain project of mind changing, misunderstanding, incomprehensible misapprehensions on which I staked my life but in such undemanding ways, not having been put to the torture for it or the flame for it or death for it, so how could I believe, how could I accept, how could I even let myself pride myself for one moment on having survived it?

And sometimes it seemed the world went, and words went, everything went but still here I was with my mind and desires often pulling in their opposite directions, chanting songs of opposition and love, yet still my mind pitched itself this way and that, as heavy as a bull's head, as empty as the barrel going over the falls with the cowardly daredevil watching with us from the shore.

I kept changing my mind, and only the voices, other voices in the street, the park, the room with me, all seeming to beckon me, calling me by my name, kept me here, kept me where I knew after everything else I should be.

PURGATORY

The purgatory of sexual failure, the memory of a time of sexual misery, sexual confusion, sexual disaster, as I imagine it must be with any purgatory, seems not the actual portion of my existence it was, but something closer to the eternity in which all existence has to reside. Surely there's nothing, at least in the years of youth, that so amputates body from mind, mind from will, and so riddles one's sense of self-sufficiency, self-regard . . .

I was quite astonished when I calculated recently how long the period of that anguish actually was, that it could be measured in months, perhaps a year, not the aeons it seems to have been at the time.

That was many decades ago as I write this, and yet it still feels like a lapse in my character that I've kept from everyone except the young woman with whom I first failed, then from the others whom I should have known not to attempt in the state of anxiety that had overwhelmed me. It began when the girl agreed to take me inside her, immediately after she'd brought me to ejaculation with her nimble fingers, twice, and it's hardly surprising now that I would have been unable to perform, but it was then. I'd been striving for so long to convince her to let me "do it," as we put it, and here I couldn't do it myself.

I'd been with women before, and had no problem, and I still don't know what the precise mechanism was that made me define myself now as incapable, but I did, and suffered from it. Each bungled attempt reinforced my woeful condition, but I couldn't give up falling in love, and falling into bed with the women with whom I was enamored.

Then it was over, I was all right, then a gap, then a failed marriage, then for several years I was flagrantly promiscuous. It's hard not to connect my sexual rampage as compensation for that vile period of defeat and despair.

Might I have overdone it, though? Once, as I was leaving a bar with a young woman, someone I knew hissed in my ear, "Man, you'll screw anything that squats to piss." That was crude, and cruel, and besides, the woman was bright and sweet and pretty, though she dressed oddly, in lacy starched dresses when everyone else was wearing jeans. Her name, too—it just came back—was striking, but I won't repeat it here.

COMPUTER GENIUS

He's calculated a system to generate new compositions by Bach. First he thought, *I wonder if I can do it?*; then, *It's entirely feasible to do it*; then, *What good would it do to do it?*; then, *But that doesn't really have anything to do with doing it*, so he does it, sets his computers to do it, and soon enough—*It's not very hard*, he thinks—he's done it.

Is there a moral issue involved, he opines? Would Bach approve the generation of more Bach? And what if I'm diluting Bach? What if, as I'm flooding the world with a synthetic Bach, Bach himself would become less substantial.

We know what he'll think next: If I don't do it, someone else will, so it's not for me to decide whether or not to do it.

Old story: I just make the experiments, the equations; I just make the bomb; I just compound the chemical that kills the trees, the bees, the breath: I myself don't make it happen.

And his computer makes its noise, and because he truly loves Bach, he all but swoons at the pleasure of overlaying the silence between Bach and Bach with more Bach.

Because truly, he'd love to *please* Bach. Truly. And to please whatever god or muse he imagines might raise all of us above ourselves to the sublime where Bach exists now, in his new rapture and delight.

THE DEATH OF BARA,

THE CHILD HERO

In our country we've never heard of him, but in the mythologies of
the French, Bara was a great hero of the Revolution, dead at thir-
teen, the subject of a number of admiring paintings. In Jean-Joseph
Weerts's work at the Louvre, one of the enemy has a war ax at Bara's
chest, ready to plunge it into his flesh; he hesitates, though, as if he
wanted to register well this hero, who looks as unlike Rimbaud at
thirteen as might be imagined, but who still, at least in my erratic
history, painfully resembles him.

Another enemy soldier, standing behind the boy, has his sword
ready to slice into a site over the collarbone that offers a shorter route
to the innards: he, too, seems to hold back a bit, a beat, then it will
happen, the blade will plunge into this body, past this face that glows
out in a rage like a child's, with none of the decadence and decline
Rimbaud's body must have suffered from his various dissipations.

A youth who looked like and unlike Rimbaud, a tribe of enemy
soldiers, irate, disgusted perhaps to have to waste time and energy
on a probably sham hero, but noticing anyway that something had
to be noticed: that the boy, head pulled back to steel himself for the
one blow, is about to receive another he doesn't know is coming to
him from the rear. In the background, horses, other heroes, some

wounded, too. The war far off in the distance, with its tumult and reports, its cries of agony winding like Roland's horn, subdued spectators moving from one corpse to another, and unseen, in some hidden corner of the mind half a century later, might be Rimbaud, no tears in his eyes, no sadness, only the about-to-be-stifled cry in his heart for the illusion-plagued victims who in their stubborn pride still call themselves human beings.

In another image of Bara, by Moreau-Vauthier, he's a barefoot drummer boy still clutching his drum in death, a much lower-level hero myth. Yet another, by David, has him nude, writhing on the earth, his hand over a gruesome wound in his chest, the rest of his body erotically untouched, innocent, the victim of something of which he seems utterly ignorant. One thinks Rimbaud again, his crippling gift, his own plunge towards death.

WORDS

One night, in the worst days of uncertainty back in the grinding beginning of being a poet, when nothing was happening, nothing materializing on my desk but obviously incompetent crap, I had a dream, one of those intricate, leaping narratives that go on and on and on, but it was entirely in words, no images, no "characters," no places, just words, files of words, ranks of words, stumbling along one after the other.

It was a nightmare, and it frightened me. I had to struggle to come awake, and when I did, I found myself piercingly depressed.

I fell back to sleep, though, and had another dream in which I was recounting to a real poet—I wasn't sure who it was, perhaps Keats, perhaps Baudelaire; I couldn't make out any visual details; the poet, the guardian poet, I feel like calling him, was just a shape before me—but he was speaking to me, telling me he'd once had exactly the same dream himself. I was immediately relieved, but then, to my disappointment, he began to inform me what had been wrong with my version of the dream: it was badly shaped, bulky, unruly— I hadn't configured it properly, I'd have to do it again.

"Try it this way," the poet offered, but he didn't suggest anything specific, just waved his hands up and down and around like an orchestra conductor, then he said, "Read more, and we'll work on it again."

Work on what? I thought, and felt my desperation and hopelessness expanding. But when I asked him, he chuckled. "Look," he said, "we're the same person, aren't we?" and I woke again, and this time I was surprised because I was smiling, and I had the sense that someday I would be all right, I just had to be patient.

Sometimes, I'd almost say often but that wouldn't be true, it can seem I'm still being patient, still waiting, though thanks be at least not every day.

SHOCK

In Africa, on a veldt, on grass that went off into the distance like a sea, I saw in a film a fierce, determined, irresistible lion pursue an antelope fawn, cut it away from its mother and herd, run it down, catch one of those impossibly slender hind legs in its mouth ... Then everything stopped.

The fawn didn't fall but stood instead strangely still, it was "in shock," the voice-over said, and the other, watching creatures of the hot plain were motionless, too: this was taking so long, this death thing; the hair on their necks must have frozen like ice.

Then, as the lion went about its business of tearing its prey apart, everything began again: the fawn had started to fall, then it fell. Then its mother, who'd been waiting, head hanging dejectedly, fled, the herd fled, all the other animals fled, the plain was empty, only the long grass still swayed, and everything stopped again.

And I thought, This is how it is when someone dies, someone you love, how you stand still in your mind, your heart, you can't move, nothing can move, and then, as time rushes over you like the wild wind of the veldt, you come to yourself, though something within you is still fleeing, still rushing forever away, you just don't know what it is, in time's tempestuous wind it's gone, like the light in the eyes of a fawn, the light of life that doesn't easily go out but does.

A SHORT NOVEL

At the very outset of his conscious intellectual existence, when he fancied he'd begun to "think," he used to long confusedly for a vision of existence, a system—philosophical, like Hegel's, or religious, like Aquinas's, or poetic, like Dante's or Blake's—in which conceptions of cosmos and notions of human belief, morality, and action would make a coherent whole.

How he envied (although he couldn't really understand them very well) those great thinkers, their vast perceptions, their passionately comprehensible universes: spirit, history, and self fitted neatly if complicatedly together, composing a logical whole.

Little did he know he'd arrive at a point in his life at something very close to his old desire: an intuition of reality, much like those of the great generators of meaning in which everything would have its place, but it was a vision too often bleak, hopeless, stinking of despair.

A cosmos without ultimate meaning, a public world corrupt with violence and lies and the avid ingestion of lies, with only the briefest flashes of respite. All that had once seemed ephemeral distractions, ultimately trivial, off the point—family, love, art—were what kept the life of mind from annihilating negation.

POETS

When I marked up with my red felt-tipped pen the last poem my longtime poet friend had sent me, I meant to demonstrate again my allegiance, sharing his poem as for so many years we'd shared the labor we both loved.

When he decided—I've never fathomed the reason, or reasons—he wanted to terminate our friendship, he did it by slashing the draft of a poem I'd sent him with his own thicker scarlet scrawls so savagely, irrationally, with such perverse inattention, I immediately suspected he was informing me our friendship was over, and I was right. I wrote back anyway, discreetly pointing out the off-the-pointedness of most of the criticisms he'd inflicted, hoping to effect a kind of treaty between us, but he never responded, and never spoke to me again.

I suppose I'd known one day this would happen. My ex-friend had often turned on other close friends, suddenly finding them wanting, deciding they'd insulted or hurt him, and hating them. "An awful human being" is the way he'd fiercely characterize those he'd cast aside. It had always troubled me how abruptly someone could go from being one of his valued familiars to an "awful human being," but I hadn't dared mention it for fear he'd turn on me, too.

As I looked again at that sheet of paper with my vulnerable poem stained with his indelible rage, the coarse delete marks, the arrows and harsh comments, so much like blood spilling warm from a wound, I wondered if I was a little relieved that the inevitable had come to pass, that I was a member now of a certain select if unfortunate society.

But I wasn't relieved; awful human being I am, I wrote this.

LADDERS

Atom, molecule, germ, worm, serpent, bird; Australopithecus, Pithecanthropus, Neanderthal, Cro-Magnon; hunter, peasant, worker, soldier, courtier, king: this notion of *progression*, this fancied moving *upwards*, becoming worthier, more effective, efficient, more accounted for on some grander scale of value.

The illusion that one will improve, be better, if certain procedures, self-generated or prescribed by others, are adhered to, certain rigors not shirked, certain modes of application and denial vigorously implemented . . .

So much of existence seems to consist of the possibility of overcoming: practically, morally. Aren't one's own best ambitions to be put to the use of surmounting tendencies towards the trivial, the distracting?

Is everyone else condemned this way to being always haplessly embedded in one's imaginary future?

When I stop my life for a moment, when I pause the almost every moment of my life in which I need to believe I'm involved in some genre of development, I imagine all the moralists and prophets, all the speakers to the weary human soul, cajoling, commanding, hectoring, blaming.

All are involved in a conspiracy to prevent me from living a single hour with the sense of composure that would allow me to not feel that despite my efforts, which have been mostly ineffectual, I have actually slipped back even as I have striven ahead.

These ladders. These teetering, top-heavy ladders.

LISTENING

He tells her about the Mustang convertible he restored and showed at a competition in Mobile.

She tells him her father had a big yard next to their house filled with old junk that as far as she knows is still there and who can tell what crap he saved?

He tells her about the gentle Thoroughbred his uncle owned that had bad ankles and then went blind but could still find the way from the pasture to the barn right through the gate with no one leading it.

She tells him about the baby raccoon she found and raised with an eyedropper and oatmeal and how one day, half grown, it took a nap in the motor of her truck and was slashed to death by the fan.

He tells her about his son who's on track to be the youngest Eagle Scout in the history of Alabama.

She tells him that the guy who tried to feel her up in the bar last night told her he was fifty but looked twenty years older.

He tells her being married wasn't fun.

She tells him about a farmer she knows who drowns his unwanted kittens in boiling water.

Why boiling? he asks.

She doesn't know, that's what he does, is all.

YOUTH, SORROW, SYSTEM

My theory was that though others claimed they experienced *emotions*, in truth what they were speaking of were suppositions, theories, unconsidered traditions of response and retelling.

I believed emotions were actually sensations and perceptions muddled with mental projections, illusions in everything but name.

The flow of inner representations assumed forms that without reflection might be considered "emotions," but in fact the whole thing was merely convention.

Even the lust gusting through me, my love of love, my frustration, disappointment, dejection, I deemed mere intellection.

So close to desperation, kept afloat by speculations like this, I'd put them through their paces, or—and maybe I even knew it—they mine.

THE BULLY

You could see his abiding rage, his readiness to inflict pain and to suffer it if necessary to satisfy his rage, most obviously in the way he set his head on his shoulders, thrusting it forward on his neck so his skull looked even more massive than it was, and by how, when he turned to look at you, the entire apparatus, head and torso, would move too slowly, like a periscope aiming at a ship, indicating his eagerness to preemptively attack.

In any disagreement, on any subject at all, he was convinced he was correct—he'd express astonishment that you'd dare think otherwise and attempt to disagree. The willingness to hurt would invade his gaze, and unless you were ready to take him on, you'd give in, and he'd make even your surrender onerous by the way he'd watch with amusement as you scurried about behind your eyes to find ways to save for yourself what was left of your compromised valor.

Yet once you got to know him, to your great surprise, it could be comforting to be with him. Though this wouldn't make you wholly happy, you'd find yourself taking pride in your association with him; his incipient violence would become a shelter, in which you believed you could participate without complicity.

That's what stings the most in memory: your using him to but-
tress the very weakness in yourself on which he preyed. No affection
in it, no real communion, just the sanctuary human beings also find
in notions of god or race, or in those like him, with their sheltering
squints of vigilance and ire.

It would come to you much later on that you'd shamed yourself
before yourself—it was like pissing in your pants.

One day, too, you'd realize a nation, too, your own nation, could
be like that, and it too would make you feel you'd pissed yourself,
or worse.

AND I NEVER

Such a banal locution, "I never saw him again," or "her," or "them." There have been times when I've thought of someone I haven't seen for many years, tried to find her, but couldn't: an old lover for whom I still felt not any attachment, but some enduring curiosity; she was an unusual, good person, what ever became of her, how did she live her life? Or friends whose addresses and phone numbers I've lost— there's the disagreeable sensation of no longer being able to rectify having misplaced them.

The strangest thing is to discover that since I last saw someone, they've died without my being aware of it. A friend I was close to in high school, and from whom I drifted away: afterwards I no longer felt any connection to him, but there was something about his being in the world that was a part of my sense of life.

Or, odder: someone I'd admired a great deal at one point, and who had become difficult, cruel, and from whom I'd quite intentionally cut myself off. Yet when I discovered he'd died and I hadn't heard about it, I felt a grave disruption, without being able to specify precisely why.

Perhaps I never like to lose anyone, even those I might metaphorically discard. I want them to be there for me, available, however distantly, however unlikely it would be that I'd ever need them. These days, of course, with the Internet, social networks, all that, people are easier to find, but really not all that much, and going to too much trouble about it would be unseemly, a squandering of attention.

And after everything else, there's the issue of time. Would I want to know how an old lover, whom I last saw when she was twenty, would look at seventy?

Actually I would.

TELEPHONE

I come across a phrase about an undercover agent, a spy who'd been captured and tortured so viciously that he'd been "turned into a sort of human telephone," meaning his antagonists had the power now to make him confess to anything, say anything to anyone his tormentors might want him to.

Terrifying—would there be anything more devastating that could befall a human being than to have to remain alive and know you no longer owned yourself, possessed yourself, that you had become a completely malleable implement of someone else's purposes and desires?

And for a writer, we who live by and in and by means of the voice and voices of the self: it might be even more frightening for us, if there can be degrees in such appalling matters. To have your voice wrenched from the exercise of the will—what other tendrils of the soul would be torn out with it?

When we were young, and struggling to make our poems, and getting nowhere, the idea of being "spoken through," by a muse, a divinity, anything, was more than merely to be desired—it was the most seductive fantasy of all.

Vile muse! Disgusting, degrading god of voice! To come to this!

FLEXIBLE TUBING

To take my mind off the fact that I'm waiting for my doctor to call to let me know if I have lung cancer or not—Christ!—when the plumber comes today to run new water lines into the apartment we've rented and I've been renovating, I spend the day working with him, nine till five, ten minutes for lunch, exhausting, absorbing; I need the distraction.

Surely the worst thing in our new age of medicine is that you don't have to have real symptoms to be sucked into the domain of terror. You don't go in excruciating pain to the doctor and say, "Doctor cure me," and the doctor says, "You're dying, I'm sorry," and you think to yourself that at least the pain will be gone, no more suffering. In our time, we visit our physician feeling generally fine, a cold that goes on a little too long, an odd pain in the gut or rectum, and after that first innocent appointment the life you've been living abruptly ends when the doctor, armored behind his desk, assumes an unfamiliar extra seriousness and begins to discuss your possible diagnosis, X-rays, scans, endoscopies, not even bringing up yet what you know awaits you—radiation, chemotherapy, surgery . . . You nod, and nod, but you're taken by those waves of tremulous chill in the layer between skin and flesh.

The plumber is young, hardly past being an apprentice, but confident, full of himself. I help him lug in his equipment, then we tear up the floor: the moldy carpet, the dried-out slats of old hardwood, the rotted subflooring—nasty stuff. When everything's open, the inners of the walls exposed, the pipes are to be installed. The plumber does most of the work, of course, but the whole time we're together he talks to me, teaching me things: how to cut off the flow from the main, how the flexible tubing will buckle if you're not careful running it up through the wall, the correct way to solder—emery the butt, slather flux on, and touch the flame to the pipe, not the solder, which melts and runs neatly down, ringing the seam.

Then while we're taking our lunch break he begins for some reason to tell me about his marriage, six months old, and his wife, how puzzling he finds her, how she's often incomprehensibly cranky, never fixing his lunch, and how half the time when he gets home she's not even there. Then—this hesitantly, but after all, he's just making conversation, not really to me, I'm just an ear—how she prefers to watch television when he wants to make love. I just nod sympathetically, I certainly don't want to offer prognosis or counsel.

When we go back to work, he saber-saws through the last bit of flooring to make space to coax the hot-water pipe up from the riser. Then, when he gropes down into the slit to feel for the connection, his hand catches and when he pulls back, it wedges more tightly, quickly turning a bright blue, then a nasty purplish red, and begins to swell. Finally, with his other hand, he starts to shove at it, kneading it like a chunk of unfeeling beef, pushing it this way and that until it abruptly pops free.

He looks down at his hand, lying in his lap like some strangely inert little machine, which I suppose for the moment it is, then cracks it against his thigh, hard, harder, shakes it, mutters, "Well, that's not how you do that," and, no gab now, no more sharing tricks of the trade, he puts in the last length of pipe, checks for leaks, closes the cut, packs his equipment, and, not even saying goodbye, pounds downstairs out to his truck, and I suppose home to his wife.

Leaving me with that image of his hand suddenly become an inanimate object, the way my whole body is in some ways inanimate to me now that I'm alone with it again and have again to pay attention to it. The ugly, short cough chopping in my chest—had it stopped while I was working? Or did I cough and not notice?

And still the doctor hasn't called.

UNDERTOW

The first event was the exhausting trip back to shore with his daughter, who'd flown across another ocean to be with him on their vacation, and her cry, "I'm scared," and his comforting her, taking her arm more firmly in his grip, and trying to kick more strongly against the current pulling at them the other way, out. He wasn't afraid then, it was still morning, no one had realized yet there was a riptide that day, though he sensed, without fear but with concern, that something was wrong.

Normally the Mediterranean is so placid, so subservient, lapping, curling at our ankles with such agreeable domesticity that when there's a disturbance of its equanimity, when its waters manifest their kinship to the wilder, more primitive, somehow younger Atlantic or Pacific, there can almost seem to be a malevolent agency involved: all these hackles and claws of white foam aren't quite credible in themselves, there must be great fins or hands slashing at the vulnerable undersides of the waves, rising from deep beneath them to churn the frightening, unpredictable rip.

The second event was his realizing, a few hours later in the water again with still no warning of the danger, swimming towards the diving raft fifty meters out, that he wasn't going to make it, his strength was gone, then turning to look for the buoy he'd passed a few moments before, and knowing he wouldn't make that either but suddenly seeing another just strokes away, which he easily reached and hung on to, waiting without knowing he was for the third event, which was seeing his wife, who'd come out to the diving raft and now, looking for him, saw him hanging on to the buoy, resting it must have looked like, not clutching it with all his strength as he was, and her starting back towards him right into the rip he knew now was more powerful than either of them, though when she joined him, they held on for a moment, catching their breath, and during a lull made it back.

The fourth, just as they reached shore, was the woman who'd drowned, her slack, heavy, granite-gray body in the arms of the lifeguard, who himself had to be dragged to the beach by a rope around his waist.

The last, a week later, in a sudden rain squall back in the city, was, as he'd sat in his car waiting for the downpour to stop, thinking of his daughter who'd flown home a few hours before, leaving him as always aimless and depressed, waiting for the misery of being without her to settle, and seeing again, *seeing*, as clearly as it must be in what's called a vision, his daughter, hair streaming behind her as they clung to each other, smiling with her faith in him.

It was then he almost cried.

OF

That other way of being tired, when, "I'm so tired," you think, add "of . . ." and finish with whatever comes to mind, although whatever comes to mind is never really what the matter is.

Awful having the bulbs of air you breathe all be the volume of a sigh, to feel that all your lurchy, wingless stumblings have come to this, this sigh, this swaying in a state where all that counts is not to come to this, this other way of being tired, this remorseless "of . . ."

WHORES

I've been making love to every female I can get my hands on, not to his woman, though, because even in these demented days I still have a sense of honor, or I call it that, so why is my friend, my good friend, stalking towards me in the street, tearing off his tie, raging that he's going to break my head for me, my balls for me, *You treacherous shit!*

Because, I manage to calm him down and get him to tell me, his lover's confessed—confessed? lied, he means—that she's gone to bed with me and wants to leave him, and I realize I'm being used, that there's someone else she did screw whom she's hiding, and it also comes to me to wonder how she thought of *me.*

What am I, some kind of *whore*?

WHY

I've been trying to figure out why it should be that the thing that made me happiest on a day when I attended an event in New York—at which I saw some old friends plus a few people I know only slightly but in whose company I was flattered and stimulated to be—should have been a girl eight or so and a woman who could have been a hundred who both offered me the same fond smile in the subway on my way back home.

The girl was playing some sort of game with her mother in a space they were pretending was a stage behind a stairway on the subway platform. As the mother watched, the girl struck a pose the way models do in magazines, one hand on a jutting hip, the other lifted and cocked back from the wrist, and she manifested the same sexy, inviting but distant and unapproachable air real models do.

She was smiling good-naturedly at her mother—they both had long, light hair—and when she saw me watching she smiled with the same frank openness at me. The freshness of her face, the adult attitude of her body and its lithe childishness made her extraordinarily endearing. When the mother noticed, she looked over at me and smiled, too—she had as radiant a smile as did her daughter—which made the moment even more gratifying.

I came upon the old woman at the bottom of an escalator when I got off at my stop. She was African American, light-skinned, wore bright red lipstick, a red beret, and a black jacket shining with sequins, and though so elderly was still remarkably attractive. Her body was bent with osteoporosis, though, so she was very short—she had to crane her neck to look up at me—and she moved laboriously. When I stepped back from the bottom of the escalator and indicated she should get on ahead of me, she looked up at me, moved closer, and smiled the same unconditional, flirty smile the little girl had such a short while before.

When I smiled back at her, I was really smiling at them both, or all three: the girl, the mother, and this woman who could have been the mother of us all.

Precious day.

CARTS

In front of our building, early morning, before anyone else is awake, the old man who works for the city sweeping the gutters in our neighborhood and the half-derelict hermit—theatrically ragged, bearded, looking not unlike Avedon's portrait of Pound—who unofficially collates our trash, greet each other by bumping their carts, the street sweeper's wheeled trash container and the hermit's borrowed or stolen from a supermarket, nose to nose, once, then again, in the middle of the street.

An old story it must be, encountering each other, everyone else still in their warm, useless beds. Old story, together this little time, alone but not quite; not speaking, not even smiling, for this after all is serious business: how would the others get by without our immortal labor, battered old carts, primal masks of dedication and rectitude in the modest up-slant of tender rose dawn?

DAWN, SNOW

Paris is so far north—on a latitude with Labrador—that in midwinter it's still dark when I go to work, and this morning, though it rarely snows here because of the warmth from the Gulf Stream that flows over Northern Europe, light, unlikely flakes have begun to fall.

Just as I come out of our front door, a young mother hurries by, a child hanging on to each of her hands. The smaller, a boy, about three, in cute red sneakers—aren't sneakers always endearing on children of that age?—is rushing so hard to keep up that his feet in the snow glow seem to flare rapidly on and off like the signals on a fire truck.

The mother and children disappear around the corner; then, down the block, the locksmith to whom I once said hello and who hasn't forgiven me because we didn't know each other well enough for me to do that yet, looms in the shadowless gloom of his work-shop, hammering powerfully on what must be a thick slab of metal with a sharp, regular clang that in the clarified air sounds like the pulse of some savage music.

Now a handsome, well-dressed woman, thirty or so, comes to-wards me: she's delighted about something and not hiding it, strut-ting along with a kind of edgy slink that emphasizes the swing of her trim hips. She holds her head tilted a bit back, her jaws are set in a smug little grin, and though the thickening downfall pelts her face, she looks the very image of satisfaction. Wouldn't it be, to borrow a word from Hemingway, fine to know why?

Some blocks up the street, something perhaps one wouldn't care to know more about: a parked car, in the shadowed interior of which sits an unshaven man, dour, utterly immobile, with a stiffness that manifests nothing so much as just-contained rage, and, barely visible beside him, a woman whose pale hands, reflecting the outside whiteness, pick nervously at her lap as though at a knotted string or a panel of unraveling knitting, though, frighteningly, nothing's there.

By the time I get to the building where I have my study, the snow is coming down insistently, the still-dark sky is bright with it, the air tastes deliciously of it, and the two French-African girls who live here, and who every day delight me with their "Good morning we're off to school!" smiles, are out in the courtyard celebrating.

I realize it can't have been all that long since they arrived from their probably equatorial home country, so they'll never have experienced this miraculous whiteness flowing its gentle every which way down. When one notices me watching, *"Il neige,"* she calls out, *"regardez, Monsieur l'américain, il neige!"*; then they both tilt their faces up to it, open their mouths to swallow it, spread their arms and spin through it like slim propellers that will surely soon be lifted from the earth, shedding crystals of sweet, cold glee.

ADVICE

Almost directly across the street from where my son is living in an art school dormitory, long ago someone I knew jumped to his death from the back window of the top floor of a row house. An old friend, an architect who renovated the house some years ago, lives there now with his wife and son.

I mentioned this second friend in a letter to my own son the other day, because he was discouraged about not having found a girlfriend yet, and this friend had once been as shy as my son is now, until when he was forty a woman essentially bullied past his timidity and dragged him into her bed.

The ostensible reason the person who killed himself did it was that he'd been depressed, but that word carries too much random meaning—there must have been a better explanation. He was a handsome man, tall and athletic, seemingly very self-possessed, and besides that he was a doctor: he'd recently finished his internship and had just switched his residency from surgery to psychiatry. He had a girlfriend, too, although he didn't seem as committed to her as he might have been—it didn't look as though anything was particularly wrong with their relationship, it just lacked intensity.

Even back then I'd already known people who'd killed themselves—a young Dadaist artist who'd shot himself, a would-be writer who'd gassed himself in a cabin down the shore—but there was something about this death that troubled me more than the rest, because just a few days before the person did it, he and I had had a talk, and he was, in retrospect, as people used to say in those days and for all I know still may, "asking for help," and I obviously didn't offer him any, or none of any worth.

We weren't really all that close; he roomed with another friend of mine, who wasn't home when I stopped by that afternoon. A football game was playing on the television, though, the roommate was watching, and I sat down to watch for a while. After a few moments he asked abruptly, "Do you ever feel sad?"

I told him that of course I did, but, "No," he said, "I mean very sad, so that you don't know what to do about it, so that you think something's wrong with your mind."

I didn't and still don't understand why he would have been asking those questions of me, considering he hardly knew me, but I started to talk, as I tended to in those days, compulsively, with a mix of anxiety grounded in what I felt was my stupidity in so many matters, and the feeling that if I managed to say something, anything, a nugget of something true or useful might pop up in it. I told him about a bad time I'd had with marijuana a year or so before—it was one of my first drug experiences—how I'd thought I was going insane, and that even now, when I was in a room where the light was similar to what it had been when that terrifying thing happened to me, I'd feel I might be "losing it"—I still remember that was the term I used.

What did I think I was offering him? Something about the general fragility of consciousness? That if I'd come through my scary experience, and survived, maybe what he was feeling would pass, too? I don't know. When I left him, I suppose I thought I might have "helped" him, but a few days later he was gone.

He'd come home from his rounds at the hospital where he was training, taken his wallet and keys and change out of his pockets and left them on his dresser, climbed out the window, and apparently hung for a time from the sill. Then he either let himself fall or his grip gave way—I was told his fingers had left streaks on the paint— and it was five stories down into a concrete basement stairwell. Almost every bone in his body was broken, he'd lived another six or eight hours, then died. I hope he didn't come enough to consciousness to realize what he'd done to himself.

Poor man. All he missed out on. Was there something, anything, I might have said to him that could have helped? A little farther on in the touchy-feely sixties, I might have tried to embrace him, but it probably would only have threatened him then, and afterwards, too, come to think of it.

I admit I still tend to offer advice perhaps too freely, to my children, to friends—something about doing so must fortify me, make me feel better about myself. You'd think by now I'd have learned.

HEAT

An insufferably hot summer day: I'm waiting for someone I think I love to come to my room. I've been waiting for weeks, and still she hasn't come to me, but there was something about the vicious heat that though I was sweating, suffocating, rolling from side to side on my bed trying to find some less sweat-soaked spot on the limp sheets that felt a century old by then with the city's grime encrusted on them, made me in some now-forgotten way revel in my discomfort, so much so that even now more years later than I'd like to calculate I can sometimes find myself wishing I could be there again, not waiting for the woman, lord knows, she so long gone, but just being again in that stifling room in a barely oxygen-positive urban space, and knowing I was alive.

SIMON SAYS

Simon says: Jump.

I'd forgotten this game. All right there, I've jumped.

Simon didn't say to come down.

Ha.

Don't laugh, Simon says: Lust.

I do lust. I've lusted as much as I can.

Simon didn't say, Lust. Simon said, Don't lust.

How? How not lust?

Be perfect.

How be perfect? Be perfect how?

Simon says: No malice in heart. Simon says expunge.

Expunge what?

Your stupid, obstinate, fatuous self. Your gloomy, dour, sullen, despondent, wearisome self. And by the way your thoughts.

Which thoughts?

The thoughts that rage with your voice, with your words, your fear, your dread, your terror, and your roaring desire.

Why desire? I don't understand.

Simon says: Don't understand, destroy. Those parts of desire you know are liars, deceivers, swindlers, and thugs.

Help, please help.

Simon says: No help, be perfect. Simon says stamp on your useless clothes like Apocryphal Thomas, and don't dote on yourself.

I don't dote.

You do dote, and you betray.

Betray?

Because you jump, and you come down. Simon repeats. Don't come down.

I've jumped. How not come down?

Just remember, never come down, never come down.

II

CATHERINE'S LAUGHTER

CATHERINE

"How do you say it? Cat-ah-reen?"

"No, Cat-reen. And roll the *r* a little."

"Cat-ghreen?"

"Almost."

CHARLES

For quite a while after Catherine and I met, the occasion never arose for her to call me by my name, I was just "you," or "*tu*," or "*mon amour*." The first time I heard her refer to me, talking to one of her sisters, by my name, "Charles," with the French pronunciation— "Shaarl," it rhymes with "gnarl"—I was taken aback, and she admitted she had been a little, too.

We laughed about it, but even now, when she addresses me by my name instead of "*tu*," the reason has to be examined: she's irritated or exasperated with me, the distance between my tidy, compact pronoun and my gnarly proper noun pounds like a surf, and I begin to understand those cultures where everyone keeps their true name to themselves. What you let out—Charles, for me—isn't really who you are.

I forget whether in those places you ever reveal your real name, even to your loved ones, lest they betray it, but how could they do that?

HER LAUGHTER

There's no reserve, no hanging back in it, no thought of decorum, no thought of anything apparently except whatever has amused her or given her delight. It can also be splendidly . . . What? Hearty, raucous? No, those words are too coarse: her laughter always has something keen and sweet to it, an edge of something like song. It has volume, too, of course: in a group of people I can always hear her laughter soaring above everyone else's. Once, in a movie theater in New York, watching a French comedy much of the humor of which was lost in the subtitles, she laughed alone for almost the whole film, completely by herself, and never noticed.

When we first were together, I used to try to find a metaphor, a figure to specify what her laughter was like. What came closest was one of those funny, clunky wooden pull toys kids used to have, might still have for all I know—a duck, a too-long dachshund, a tiny elephant. I remember our son, Jed, had a bee, yellow and black with droll, resilient spring antennas and segmented legs.

Sometimes Jed would tug the bee behind him without bothering to look. The thing might not even be on its wheels anymore, it would just be bouncing helter-skelter, wonkety-wonk along, ricocheting onto its imperturbable nose, wobbling, rolling, bumping, snagging on cracks in the sidewalk, making brave little leaps like a salmon.

Like that her laughter was, and is, when something strikes her as funny, and she's already happy, which she almost always is—just like that, a toy a child is dragging unselfconsciously behind, just like that.

SQUELCHED

Sometimes her laugh gets squelched somewhere under her throat; it's trying to rise but she's holding it back, keeping it in its little cage.

This is when she's said something she knows is funny, and you're laughing. She tries to hold her face still, but her smile is so eager to insinuate itself into her voice that she can hardly manage it, her eyes close with it, her torso struggles not to quake, rock with it, her lips are screwed shut, then she can't do it anymore, the laughter erupts, the notes of it shine through, it's here, it's arrived.

"What a pleasure," a friend once remarked, "to make that woman laugh."

FUNNY

Jessie, my daughter, when she was eight, already the warm and loving person she still is, said to me once when Catherine was laughing about something with Jed in the other room, "Catherine laughs funny, doesn't she?"

"It's nice, though, isn't it?" I asked her.

"Oh, yes, that's not what I mean," she replied.

And Jed, when he was three and still spoke mostly French, would sometimes be uproariously amused by an English word. "Inch," when I said it to him one day, sent him into hysterics.

Catherine was in the kitchen right then and when I went in to get something, she said, "Jed has a funny laugh, don't you think?"

"What do you mean?" I asked her. "He has your laugh."

"Really?" Catherine said. "Well, if you say so."

NOT

However reckless and abandoned and contagious and unabashed her laughter might be, even when she's wholly taken by something, it's never too much. Not too much, the way, once, at a party we gave, to which a friend brought both his wife and mistress, who'd supposedly achieved a truce of some sort, the lover laughed.

The wife, that evening at least, was buying none of their ostensible truce. She occupied herself entirely and quite openly contemptuously with the other wives and girlfriends, while the mistress (she'd soon leave our friend, devastating him) sat with the men, the husbands and boyfriends, gabbing with them, laughing, shooting the shit . . .

Not that laughter, not ever for a moment that husband laughter, lover laughter, that stoical laughter that slapped its knee, elbowed your ribs, told dirty jokes . . .

I've never heard that laughter from Catherine, I hope I never have to.

REAL BEES

Jed, three or four then, and Catherine and I are watching a nature program on television about the life of insects, photographed by one of those new micro cameras—life in a hive, in a drop of water, that sort of thing. It turns out to be very funny, a trap-door spider popping up like a jack-in-the-box to grab a passing beetle, an ant ponderously hauling a mighty crumb.

We're all laughing together, but Catherine's transported. A scene with flying bees bumping into one another and falling all over themselves like incompetent little airplanes she finds hilarious, she's absolutely rhapsodic about it, each moment of the film is funnier to her than the last, her laughter fills the room, and at one point Jed and I both look away from the screen and glance at her, then we look at each other, our gazes meet briefly—Catherine still in the midst of one of her peals of delight—and something passes between us: we're caught together in some unspoken, never to be spoken of conspiracy, beyond us both.

CRAZY

Maybe it's just my age, but sometimes these days when I'm making love to Catherine it feels as though I'm really making love as much, or more—no, that's going too far, just as much—to her beauty. Is this unusual? Unhealthy? I have no idea. When I tell Catherine, she says she never thinks of herself as beautiful.

That's crazy, I say, you're fibbing.

No, she insists . . . Then, she admits, maybe once. When she was sixteen or so, in a resort town somewhere with her parents, she noticed people looking at her differently from the way they always had. She went back to her room and looked into the mirror, and she did indeed look beautiful to herself.

That's the only time, though.

Ha, I say: What about when O—— tried to kiss you? What about when M—— tried to hold your hand?

She laughs. Okay, maybe once or twice.

Ha. Once or twice. Ha.

HER BEAUTY

Men often find Catherine beautiful, and besides that the kind of beauty she has seems to make them feel free to tell her. "Beautiful," said a normally quite reserved, not to say quite often irascible sociologist friend when he met Catherine on the first walk she and I took when we came from Paris to Philadelphia. I introduced Catherine; he looked at her, shook her hand, and said it: "Beautiful." Just like that, not "She's beautiful," not "You're beautiful," just "Beautiful."

Which might seem odd, except it's precisely what a very unreserved poet, well known for his exuberance, said too, also shaking her hand, when he met Catherine at one of his readings: "Beautiful."

Some other friends, too, a painter, another poet, same thing: "Beautiful," just like that, just that.

And I guess I should mention the famous man I won't name here who didn't say "beautiful" when Catherine and I met him at a conference, but who, I found out from her after he died, had tried, unsuccessfully thank goodness, to convince her to come to his hotel room. I, as vigilant as I am—I really am, because I'm so fearfully jealous—suspected nothing, which I'm glad about now because we came to cherish the man later as a friend, and it would have been difficult for me if I'd known.

The strangest thing is when I first met Catherine, I didn't think of her as all that beautiful. Nice-looking, certainly, pretty; but not really beautiful. I've often wondered why, but I can't remember, and I can't remember either when I did start thinking of her as beautiful. When we first met—it was at Kennedy Airport, our plane to Paris was ridiculously late—she was standing patiently in the line of passengers, and smiled in commiseration at me, I suppose already recognizing my pain-in-the-neck impatience. She was dressed, I remember perfectly, in a schleppy, shapeless black sweater, not very flattering jeans, and wore big eyeglasses. I smiled back but moved away because I was trying to find out what the hell was going on and the airline people were being very unhelpful.

After a few hours we were told the plane still hadn't arrived from Europe but that we'd be taken out to dinner. A bus came, I got on, and Catherine sat beside me. We didn't get to Paris for another day and a half, and by then we were friends, and soon after and ever since lovers.

Back to her beauty. I've been in quite a few situations when someone we don't know will look across a dinner table, say, and I'll realize that Catherine's beauty has suddenly dawned on them. There's always a slight look of surprise in their expression, almost shock, as though a light had been turned on around her. And that's just what it's like: when Catherine becomes interested in something, animated, involved in a conversation, an idea, an emotion, she takes on a kind of glow. I really can't explain it: she's just all at once beautiful, to me more beautiful.

I enjoy when that happens, when people—I purposefully don't say "men" because it happens with women, too—will fall in something like love with her. Sometimes, if the person is an attractive male, it doesn't make me terrifically happy. As I say, I'm painfully jealous, but I survive.

JEWELS

Catherine and I, a few days after we met, are taking a walk on one of the fanciest, most upscale streets in Paris. We pass by the most elegant of all the jewelry stores—money all but drips from the facade.

"I once had a bracelet from there," Catherine remarks.

"Where is it now?" I ask her.

"I sold it to pay for my divorce."

"Who gave it to you," I ask, "your ex-husband?"

"No."

"Who then?"

"An admirer."

"An *admirer*?"

She'd never say who.

JEALOUSY

I try, without immediately laughing aloud, to consider seriously the proposition that Catherine might be jealous of *me*. I make a little psychic drama in which I'm in conversation with someone, anyone, it doesn't matter, and that she's looking across at me and smoldering, quavering, dissolving with anxiety and fret.

Utterly impossible. She couldn't know, couldn't suspect, couldn't have the wildest imagination of what it would be like.

Here's what it's like: I'm watching her, at a party, say, a restaurant, a gallery, conversing with another man, someone she evidently admires, perhaps feels affection for, perhaps, I think, incipient love for, sexual passion for. Of course I keep my mouth clamped, sealed, hammered, nailed, screwed shut.

When I consider what to do next, the only solution I can posit is to become inanimate, and the shortest route to that would be to become one with the chair in which I sit. My all at once beloved chair: its back is almost precisely the length of my spine, and its seat—think!—has more legs than I have! What relief! I am the chair that holds me, that holds me up. I am chair.

But now an army of ravenous invisible birds approaches the foot of the cherished chair to harvest the crumbs of my psyche as it disintegrates and dissolves. Secret birds: their eyes shine like the nails of a nurse preparing for your operation.

Then the crumbs are gone, devoured, there's nothing left of me, psyche, body, brain, and so the birds, in a disanesthetizing gleaming shudder fly away.

It goes on . . . I wait, I watch, I count, my heartbeats, my brain waves, but the chair is growing tired, it bends one leg, then another. My chair, poor chair, it doesn't even have eyelids to swing down like shutters . . . Or do I mean shudders?

What do I mean? I forget what I might mean, or anything might mean. I find I envy now the placid, stupid foursquare tables, then the lamps that perch on them and burn, burn if they desire all the endless night.

Like them, I burn, I watch, with something like a mighty winch I haul my eyes agape and watch.

FASTER

When the workmen came to unclog the cesspool of the tiny house in Greece Catherine and I had rented those first weeks we were together, they heaved the syrupy shit-gunk into the shallow cove in front of our terrace, and it settled through the vividly clear water into a gray layer on the rocks and pebbles at the bottom and stayed there.

The reason they did it was because the water that fed the house had been contaminated, but it was even more foul now—we couldn't drink it, cook, or even shower with it. There was a well, though, a little way up the hill behind us, and we'd walk there with a big ceramic jug to rinse ourselves off. The water was clean, but icy cold— I hated it.

Catherine appeared not to mind, but when I'd pour the water over her head and it would run down over her body, her skin would erupt in goose bumps—what a crude term for such a lovely phenomenon—and she'd all at once possess a different sort of corporality, solidity, depth.

"Breathtaking," another absurdly inadequate word, but my breath really would be taken—I'd gasp, my breathing would stop, then start again, faster, faster.

PAINTING

Catherine and I are renovating our new apartment and for the last four days I've been scraping off wallpaper, the worst job on earth, the most repetitive and boring, and all the while Catherine's been busy with other things, taking care of Jed, going to her job at a jewelry workshop, so she hasn't been here at all, it's been just me hour after hour with the miserable steaming machine and the clumsy putty knives. We've agreed I'll take the afternoon off for some work chores I have to finish by tomorrow, and she's already ten minutes late.

Now she's finally here. I hear her key at the door, hear her footsteps in the hallway, hear her come to the room, and there she is. She's dressed in old sneakers, worn jeans, and an old down jacket of mine which it goes without saying is much too big for her, so she has the air of a kid dressed up in adult clothes, and also she's carrying a paper bag the contents of which I can't figure out.

"Voilà, here I am," she says, looking around at the scraps of ancient wallpaper and the fragments of old molding on the grimy carpet. I'm impatient for her to get to work, though, and she knows I am—the whole atmosphere of the room is declaring, "Let's get to work." But first . . . Out of her mysterious bag she plucks . . . What?

Her radio, for goodness sake, her ridiculous out-of-date radio, and she holds it up, even though we both know the time's past for screwing around, and says, "Where's the plug?"

"Where's the damned plug?" is what I want to answer, but when I look at her she looks suddenly like Charlie Chaplin, or maybe Stan Laurel, and she knows it, and knows too that I know it and we both know how silly this is and how sweet—it's a scene from some comic movie, and we both must think that at the same instant so that after a pause just the duration Chaplin would have been pleased with I get off the ladder, embrace her, and we laugh, and kiss, I leave, and yes, she really does get to work so that when I come back a few hours later she's scraped the paper off the whole dining-room ceiling, a task I'd been dreading—it's an offering for me from her, as though I needed another.

ANNIVERSARY

"It's not so bad all the time being married to you," Catherine tells me.

"You mean it's not bad being married to you all the time."

"No, I mean it's not bad all the time being married to you."

LATER

It must have been after some intense discussion, not an argument, nothing personal, just my usual gloom erupting, that Catherine wrote in pencil on a sheet of "While You Were Out" paper that I came across in a pile of papers months later, long after I'd forgotten what we might have been disagreeing about: "Differ without rancor as a man may differ with himself . . ."

I have no idea where she found the quote, but underneath it, in blue ink in my hand, is written: "I differ from myself with rancor."

Then in pencil under that, in her writing again, "You're stupid, that's why."

MISCARRIAGE

When we had the miscarriage, that fearsome middle-of-the-night bleeding, frantic calls to the doctor—"Rest . . . Wait . . ."—then so much blood, gouts splattering the floor, the bed and sheets soaked . . .

When, after the surgery, Catherine came back, she couldn't or wouldn't wake from the anesthesia. The surgeon kept urging her, "Wake up now, open your eyes!" flicking a fingernail on the side of her hand, but her eyes stayed sealed, she seemed to be hardly breathing, and finally the doctor told me to try.

I was frightened—how much she must have wanted to stay where she was, how reluctant to come back—but I tried: "Open your eyes, love . . . *Faut te reveiller . . .*"

Her lips moved a little, her eyelids fluttered almost imperceptibly.

"Okay," the doctor said, "let her sleep now," and she did sleep, for hours and hours while I waited for her to wake again.

DANCE

Catherine studied ballet when she was young; she never talks about it, but once, in the most boring room of a depressing museum in Denmark, she suddenly whirled three perfect piqué turns across the floor and ended up out in the corridor, ready, to my relief, to leave.

PERFUME

Catherine is drying herself off after her bath; she has a tiny vial of perfume and she dabs some on the back of her neck.

"What's that?" I ask her.

"Come here," she says. "They gave it to me in a store, it's for men."

She puts some on my hair.

"Not on my hair," I say, "it stinks."

I take the vial. It's called Yatagan, or some crap like that. "Look," I say, "even the name is ridiculous."

"Well," Catherine says, "we'll find some perfume for you with a nice virile name."

"Like what?" I ask.

"How about Dung?" she answers.

"Dung?" I say. "*Dung?*"

Catherine laughs. "Close the door."

SULKING

We've been spatting and sulking and brooding and sizzling; I go teach my class, come home, Catherine's at her workbench, and though it's not easy, "I'm sorry," I say. "I was really depressed, I just wanted some solace."

Catherine's still angry: "Maybe I'm depressed, too," she answers. I'm stunned, then angry again. "What should I say?" I ask her. "That I was first, that I was depressed first?"

Catherine turns her head away from me; then after a moment I notice that her shoulders seem to be shaking a little. For a moment I can't tell for sure what's going on: she's not saying anything, but more of her body is shaking, and then it breaks through, her laughter, she's laughing. I'm saved! Free!

I touch her, she leans back against me, laughing; her body against me has such solidity now, I can feel the muscles in her shoulders, the flat bones on her back moving under my hands—those "wings," we call them, as we should.

TUESDAYS

When some friends left their two daughters, seven and five, with us to take care of for a few hours, Catherine told them stories, two of her favorite fairy tales. One I hadn't heard before was about a king who falls in love with a beautiful princess who agrees to marry him on one condition: that on Tuesdays she has to be alone—he can't see her or talk to her, she just has to be allowed to stay by herself in her room.

The king agrees, they marry, they're very happy, except that the king becomes curious, then obsessed, as we will, by what in heaven's name could be going on on Tuesdays in that room, and one day he breaks open the door to see. When he enters, his wife looks at him sadly, turns into a blackbird, and flies out the window.

The king is devastated, needless to say, and in the original, that's the end of the tale—I suppose the moral is, don't be so nosy, something like that.

But when Catherine tells me about telling it to the girls, she felt she had to add a different ending: one day the king is moping in tears through his estate and another blackbird approaches him and asks him what's wrong. He confesses the error he'd made and the blackbird tells him he'll have another chance, that he should go home.

He goes back to his palace and there's his wife again waiting for him. He's overcome with joy, and they live happily ever after.

Except, of course, Catherine laughs when she tells me, on Tuesdays.

TALK

Catherine and I, for some long-forgotten reason, have both been irritable all day, touchy, preoccupied, moody, and gloomy. Dinner is peaceful, though, and when we finish Catherine asks, "Are we going to make love tonight?"

I answer, "If I'm talking to you."

"You don't have to talk," Catherine says.

BREEZE WITH FLOWERS

A puff, and the flowers jerk in erratic little spasms, as, when we make love, her body will sometimes move gently to no rhythm. A larger gust then and they spin at the limit of their attachment, until, becalmed, they're released back into their decorous stillness, as when, after, she is often taken by an engrossing, enviable calm.

The breeze again: the flowers all lean in the same direction, like sopranos reaching for a note (and aren't they, the flowers, voices without singers, exalting with and to one another in their fragrant silence?), as her voice becomes other than voice, more than voice, finds more voices in her voice.

Beneath, the leaves and stems shuffle together, like corps of violinists, dutiful, dedicated, constant, then are still again, as I, dedicated, constant, lie beside her now, constant, stilled.

THE FIRST TIME

The first and I'd wager the only time I'll ever fall asleep laughing, Catherine and I had been making love earlier in the evening and lost track, so to speak, of our route, and tipped off the bed onto the floor. Such a tangle of limbs and buttocks bouncing on the hard wood, but Catherine of all things began laughing and kept laughing for a bit even after we were back in bed, but she'd hit her head on the bedside table and when we got up for dinner she had a swelling on her forehead, which she put ice on, and some French homeopathic gunk she believes in.

Then, later, when we went to bed, I reached over I thought very gently to pat her head to see how she felt, but just then she moved towards me so that my hand bumped right onto where she was bruised, and, "So," she said, "are you going to attack me again?" and burst out laughing, and what else could I do but laugh, too, and we both couldn't stop, lying there laughing, laughing together as we held each other and drifted away.

DOGS

When she walks our dog, Catherine tends to be a bit oblivious to how much mischief Bwindi might effect. She lets her wander at the end of her leash, even in the middle of town; sometimes the leash will get entangled around people's legs, and once Bwindi snatched a croissant out of the hand of a baby in a stroller. The baby howled, Catherine was very embarrassed and offered to buy another, but the amused mother declined.

When Catherine tells about that, she laughs, but recently there was a more dramatic incident. She was walking through the town near where we live when we're in France, and a woman, when she saw Bwindi approaching on her loose leash, stopped dead on the sidewalk, obviously frightened. Catherine noticed, brought Bwindi against her legs, and asked the woman what was wrong. The woman responded that she had a terror of dogs: she was Jewish, and when she was four during the war, German soldiers came with police dogs and took away her parents and brother and sister and she never saw them again.

Hardly surprising she wouldn't care for dogs. She and Catherine chatted awhile and the woman told how she'd been saved when she'd been left alone in Paris, that she'd been sent to be brought up by a couple here in this town where she still lived.

Some years ago I saw a show in a museum of photographs of French people who had helped Jews during the Nazi frenzy, taking them into their homes, hiding them, bringing them up as their own children. I wanted to write about it, but nothing I could say came close to doing justice to what was visible in the saved and saviors in those pictures: their simple, factual presences, no glow, no halos, nothing exalted in their expressions. They were real, as we all are, and that was enough.

In this case, though, it didn't turn out so well. The woman had been very unhappy with the couple who'd adopted her, and had had what sounded like a generally unfulfilling life.

Catherine was moved—that's not the way you want stories like that to end. But even the beginning ... Catherine was only a few years younger than the woman; they'd both been born in Paris, perhaps blocks from each other. If Catherine had been a Jew ...

There are matters that can't be coped with in reflecting on life, or love, or sometimes it seems anything at all.

LOOBAHSH

Catherine reads a lot, and quickly, and often listens to authors on the radio, both in France and in the States, then buys their books. Though very few turn out to be as interesting as their authors have made them sound, this doesn't deter her, she still listens, and buys, and reads.

When she brings a book to bed, as she always does before we go to sleep, she puts her feet up on the wall over the headboard. As she reads, one heel will rub lightly over the shin on her other leg, then go out straight so her legs are parallel again, lines ending in infinity, I think. Then the other leg will bend, move against the first, straighten out again and aim again.

Tonight, earlier in the evening we'd watched a DVD of a Hungarian movie, very stark, gloomy, about starving peasants, a father and daughter, and the peasants' broken-down, ill horse, and also, the last moments of the film implied, though you couldn't be certain, the end of the world. Much darkness, much raw fear.

There was very little dialogue, mostly single-word ejaculations the father and daughter passed between them and almost all of which were subtitled as "Fuck!" Their horse is dying: "Fuck!" Their well has run dry: "Fuck."

Later, Catherine in bed reading, me getting undressed, something falls clattering from her bedside table, Catherine mutters, "Fuck!" and I say, "That's what they said in the movie."

And Catherine, who didn't care for the film and watched only parts of it, says without looking up from her book, "Loobahsh."

"What?" I ask. "Is that the word?"

"Loobahsh," she says again, a grain of laughter in her voice.

"You made that up," I say to her. "Very funny."

Again, with a chuckle, "Loobahsh . . . Loobahsh."

Her left heel runs over her right shin, she flexes her foot then straightens her knee so her legs are parallel again, both aiming once more towards the planets and stars.

OAKS

After dinner, still at the table, I'm writing in my little notebook, scribbling fast, when Catherine says she'd like to take a walk. When I tell her I'm busy she takes the empty dishes into the kitchen, then comes back.

"Come on, take a walk."

"I'm writing," I tell her.

"Take your notebook. You can take your wine, too."

"Wait just a minute," I say.

"You need a bigger notebook," Catherine says then. "I'll buy you a bigger notebook."

"I don't need a bigger notebook, and don't get me one."

"That's why I said it," Catherine says. "I just wanted to hear you say that. Let's go for a walk."

Finally I give up, give in, we stroll out across the park near our house and come to the pair of gigantic old oaks Catherine particularly loves. The trunk of each tree is about five feet across, and they stand close together, leaning a little as though making room for each other.

They're in full-leaved gorgeousness right now, and when we get to them Catherine says, "You have to come in here," and leads me between them.

"Now close your eyes," she says.

"Why?"

"Because there are all those branches above us," she answers, "and beneath us the roots. You have to listen."

I listen. "But I don't . . ." I start to object.

"You have to come stand here every day, then you will," Catherine answers, not laughing now. "You'll see, you will."

III

CODES

When the Rothschilds were accumulating their vast fortunes, and even after, they wrote their confidential business letters to other members of the family in code. Furthermore, these secret letters were not only written in the usual descending lines down the page, but the messages would also continue across the page in the other direction, making them essentially impossible for anyone not in the family to read.

How much of a factor the indecipherability of the letters actually was in the amassing of their empire, I have no idea, but I find it impossible not to think here of Robert Walser, the great Swiss author, writing, after he had gone insane, what are called now (though he never did) "microscripts," described by their translator as "narrow strips of paper covered with tiny, antlike markings ranging in height from one to two millimeters . . ." It was thought at first that they were nonsense, generated by the schizophrenia that had sent him to an asylum in 1929, where he would remain until his death, in 1956, but then they were deciphered. Some of them were written on the back of peoples' calling cards, some on the pages of tear-off calendars *which he'd cut in half* before he'd begin to write.

In a further complication, at some point he decided that pens had become his enemies, he could no longer trust them. Not daring to compose with them, he turned to less dangerous pencils, always very small ones. Painstakingly sharpened they must have been, those simple gadgets of graphite and wood, to be able to make such intricate inscriptions on those scraps as humble as the rags of desert saints.

I've always been struck by the raging commercial single-mindedness of the Rothschilds—but Walser, what passion, what devotion, and with writing tools that for all he knew were secret spies, secret foes.

MYTH

In one version he'd have left her soon after he met her, but she was teaching him ways past the quicksand and crypts, the dead ends he came to think would undo him without her.

In another it was the vein of obligation spun seemingly out of her bosom that held him: he roved and raged, raged and roved, but it still bound him to her.

The episode of his confession has her scouring his psyche with caustic correctives: she so comprehended his flaws, could so explicate his weaknesses—how could he not stay with her?

Finale and coda: out past the monsters of conscience, through labyrinths of guilt and contrition, detested, envenomed, he found himself back in the world beyond myth; no longer merely paroled but—he hardly knew what to do with himself—free.

THEY CALL THIS

A young mother on a motor scooter stopped at a traffic light, her little son perched on the ledge between her legs, she in a gleaming helmet, he in a replica of it, smaller, but the same silvery color and just as shiny. His visor is swung shut, hers is open.

As I pull up beside them on my bike, the mother is leaning over to embrace the child, whispering something to him, and I'm shaken, truly shaken, by the wish, the need, to have those slim, strong arms contain me in their sanctuary of affection.

Though they call this regression, that implies a return to some past state, and this has never left me, this fundamental pang of being too soon torn from conditions of bliss that promise ever more bliss, no matter that the scooter's fenders are pimpled with dents, nor that as it waits, it pops impatiently, clears its throat, growls.

CONFLICT

The adversarial relationship I have with myself: I think something, I oppose it; I "feel" something (although I'm still not sure what that precisely means), I reject it. How weary I am of it, how condemned I seem to be to it. When I think of trying to change, it seems I'd have to become someone else entirely.

How did it begin? How did I come to feel the most virtuous way for me to live was by constantly opposing myself, questioning myself? Often, when I have these impulses I put them down to the fact that I'm "spoiled," that I've lived with too many privileges, too abiding well-being and insufficient sensitivity to offset them. I tell myself I have to come to terms with these elements of myself, which, in some depressing way, are myself.

I know this is where I situate myself morally, but psychologically there has to be more to it. I have no wish to subject myself to the schematics and repetitiveness of Freudian reasoning, although it was in the past useful to me, or so I think. But was it really? Am I sure? Might there be other misconceptions about myself that have driven me to believe this? If I were to really examine my experience with the analytic modes I've ingested, absorbed, would I find that they've benefited me, or have they in fact only led me to this divided way of thinking about myself, and to my having faith that such re-flections are virtuous?

But is this (I refer to this whole complex of thoughts and feelings now as "this") finally part of the very foundation of my character as I live it? All this, in fact, can seem to be something that came upon me at the particular moment in my life when I undertook to be what I understood was a human being, something for which I realized I had no recognizable qualifications, and so was thrust into a nearly constant state of feeling myself illicit, illegitimate, unentitled.

I accepted this conflict, perhaps, as a part of what my becoming an adult had to entail. It was, in some ways, the only thing of which I could be certain. If one says to oneself, and believes, "I am an amoral clod," one can only rise in one's own (more important than in others') estimation. In a sense, one has already failed, so how fail more?

Yet surely there's much in the world beyond myself that needs this kind of reflection: in fact nearly everything else. But how dare dream of speaking for one's culture, of collating the aspirations and successes or failures of one's moment of history, when one is so worn down generating a mode of being for oneself? Wouldn't such speculations embody timidity and fear?

Maybe all this has to do with how attached one can become with-out being terribly aware of it to the conditional, both the possible and the not probable, in either of which what might be coming now would be greater and grander than what there is now. But doesn't such commitment to the conditional make the fragile moment I exist in now, suspended over chasms and abyss, seem a more meager sort of tense, a mere "present," compared with some imperative in which everything would become something other than incipience or incubation?

And yet after all of this, this grinding, this abrading, there are moments, more than moments, when the world's facticity, its utter simplicity, is intensified, enhanced, as though I've become something like a lens ground finer than I'd realized. I behold the world as it is, its volumes, its space, its people and things: I see all glowing in the astonishment of existence. Reality isn't dimmed, diminished, thrown out of focus by my struggle with myself; it's clarified, and if at first what I draw from that vividness, that blaze, is fret, concern, anxiety for it as for myself, still I hold on, I keep it all, or try.

WOMEN

I feel as though I've always been all but fatally susceptible to the beauty of women. Since I've been with Catherine and have experienced the once unforeseeable pleasures of fidelity, I haven't acted on my condition—that's what I believe it is—but I remain stricken by the emanations of female beauty that so charge the reality in which I exist.

I walk through the streets of a city—women all over the place, everywhere. This one is beautiful, I note, this one a bit less; this one overwhelming, this other merely painfully seductive.

Then, on some days, especially if I happen to have beheld many of them, they *all* become beautiful: the slim, the hefty, the "well-built," and the less endowed—young and old they flaunt themselves before me and for me, they enchant me and exhaust me.

I'm dizzy with it. I'd close my eyes in ecstasy, but I know I might stumble and fall and one of them would stop to help an old man to his feet, and where would I be then, old man, helpless, shameless old man?

BOOKS, DAMNED BOOKS

Remarkable how quickly the books pile up in my room, on my desk, on the table behind it, on the long, low cabinet already filled with papers of every sort—half-finished poems, ruined essays, old bills, beckoning tax papers, and, on top of it all, books, volumes of poems, stories, theories, histories, translations, and of course more on the bookshelves, though I rarely glance at them, and those on the shelf over my desk, which compose my canon of essentials and which I often find myself scanning to bring me out of a silence.

The whole house, come to think of it, seethes with books, but those in my room seem particularly animate, alive, an accumulation like cells dividing. But still, as each new one arrives—a translation of a Yiddish poet I'd never heard of, someone's *Selected* or *Collected*, or a new edition of a great unknown—I feel comforted, protected by them, my eyes have somewhere to travel when they wander from the blank paper instead of out the window where, in truth, at least this moment (well, maybe many moments), I'd really rather be.

Then there are the days when all my beloved books become oppressive, weigh on me, it can feel with the literal poundage of their paper and cardboard and cloth; they seem almost to claw at me with their figurative shouting and beckoning and demanding. Read me, understand me, find the proper place in your life for me, when you do you'll be complete . . . Complete?

Time to leave, to get out. In another epoch and another literary mode I might run out of the room, rush into the street, throw myself under a trolley or truck, but now I just long to be somewhere without books, without *books*. How believe myself, though, when I well know that soon I'll be over this attack, this spasm, this fit?

BOMBS

A theory I developed about nuclear bombs, in the months it would have been after the confrontation between the United States with the Soviets over Cuba, that unthinkable week when we really believed the end might be upon us, when being consumed in clawing flames or dissolving in invisible poison was what awaited us.

This was a bad enough time in my life already. I was struggling to write a decent poem, and hadn't yet; I was uncertain about myself, about what I was doing with myself, whether I'd perhaps made some misguided and irrevocable choices. I suppose it was just normal, trite young artist crap, but it's impossible now not to connect the turmoil I was going through, the struggle I thought was all my own, with the horrors that afflicted all humanity, these technologies we'd devised before which we were impotent, and awed.

I still don't know how serious I was about my idea, whether it may have just been something I used to startle other people, but the notion I came up with was that all history from the beginning of time has been driven by a hunger for beauty, by an evolving passion for the beauty we could produce and add to the aesthetic dimension of existence, which was what the human race was really all about. A nuclear bomb going off, that inconceivable flash of flame—the

Jovian clouds frenziedly boiling from its base, then the towering column and crown of steam, smoke, pulverized earth, wood, steel, flesh—had to be the most beautiful object humans had ever brought into being.

Our evolution, therefore, had been consummated: the planet, the universe, even god if there was one had need of us no longer, and in the unexplored parts of ourselves we knew it. The chilling obeisance we felt beholding the bomb had fear in it, yes, but also exaltation, our realization beyond any mode of analysis that our devising of such a spectacle, however vile, was triumph, not defeat.

HIM

Something I still wonder about: a woman I once had a thing with, whose previous lover when she told him said, "Oh, no, anybody but him."

Why that? Why "Anybody but him"?

It wasn't that they were still close, they'd split a good while before; she even showed me a scar on her forehead where he'd hit her with an iron.

So why anything at all, no less "Anybody but him"?

She was white, he was black, naturally I thought it might be that, but he didn't say, "Anyone but a white man," he said, "Anybody but *him*."

Was it because I'd been involved as he had with not a few other women, including one I knew he'd cheated on this one with?

But why would that bring him to "Anybody but him"?

Well, whatever became of them both, I hope they found what they needed.

Still, I'd rather neither remembered his having said, whatever his reason, "Anybody but him."

THIGHS

The very great, very tall, truly out of human scale basketball player has been injured—"a deep thigh bruise"—and all his many fans including I admit me are worried: How can he play, as he puts it, at a hundred percent when it hurts to walk, not to say leap; if he can't even leap, how can his team not suffer defeat?

I leave the sports page, return with reluctance to page one, and read (I couldn't bear to before) about a taxi driver in Afghanistan, a small man, five two, arrested by mistake, hung by his wrists, and . . . tortured. They don't want to say it, but he was tortured, by blows of his U.S. soldier-jailers' knees to his legs, violent blows, countless deep, bruising blows, hateful even to think it, for days, again and again, and his tormentors, instructed to do this, obeyed, because, they were given to think, this wasn't torture, torture is something with chains or flame: torture, they're told, "is something people like us don't do."

But then the obstinate taxi driver, who'd never confess he'd done anything wrong, because he hadn't, did, do something wrong: he died, of blood clots risen to his heart from the crushed arteries in his thighs—his thighs, said the doctor who performed his postmortem, had been "pulpified." "Pulpified!" like ground meat.

This week, with time to rest his injury (a "charley horse," we called it when I played, it did hurt a lot), the very great player is feeling stronger. "I'm at eighty percent of my game," he reports to the press, and indeed his team wins, in a rout. I don't remember the score, but that's how the paper put it, "a rout."

A JEW, A ROAD, SOME CROWS

"I am dying of the itch," he thinks; a wheel jolts in a rut, the plank seat slaps at him, "or of this wretched cart," he thinks, kicking the mare's gaunt haunch, "or of the stink. Father in heaven, cure me of my wretched stink, cure me of my itch, cure me, Father, of whatever next affliction you have stored up in your stinking palace of a hell for me."

Fallow fields, a road that winds out listlessly ahead, pricking the horizon, vanishing; east and west stripped winter trees, lowering clouds, a frozen river; crows.

"Who has called me back," he thinks, "who has brought me back to toil along this road, to watch these crows that wait for me to die so they can eat the eyes I loathe them with? Who would bring me back through these erasures and annihilations, my oblivion, my sleep? Once I slept, now I can't remember if I peddled rags or grain or air, or if I starved or ate."

A village, oiled paper windowed huts, roofs leaking rain, doors leaking wind; a dark that spreads like thickening oil over the bitter snow; the cold, the crows.

"Whoever called me back, let me go again. What meaning can I have for you? Do you mean to mourn? Who? Me? Yourself? Am I the one who'll let you mourn your dissipating history, your self thinned out of all but mythlessness and waste? Am I to be your lens? What other meaning will I have, peddling wheat or rags or gold?"

Konskiwolie, Mazelbožec, Korznice, Glisk. Between them fallow fields, rutted roads, bitter cold. A Jew, a road, some crows.

LOST BOY

If you asked where he was staying, he'd answer: "Nowhere." If you insisted, he'd answer: "I don't have a place." By "place" he meant *place*. He meant any place. He meant a room, corner of a room, square foot, square inch.

Sometimes he had food stamps, sometimes not. Sometimes welfare, maybe not. Nobody knew why yes or why no.

He had "clients" (that was his word) he serviced in their cars. Fewer and fewer, but some. Did any ever take him "home"? Seemingly not. Not any, not some.

Sad to remember the father and mother. They fought, fought. Not the way we fight; they fought like maniacs, beasts. Then they split. Came together, fought, split, and died. Both suddenly died.

He was eleven, it must have been, mother and father both gone.

Some aunt and uncle in another state took him in, until he was a certain age, sixteen or eighteen, who knows? He'd became difficult, duplicitous, quarrelsome, destructive, and so was kicked out, ejected.

He moved his life into the streets. Did this, that. Who knows?

An old friend of his parents took him in once, he stayed a few weeks, ate, watched TV, hung out, but stole, money, money and dope, and more money. The friend turned him out, too. Back to the street.

When you ask where he is now, one person will tell you he's dead, and though she hates to say it, she's relieved, she'd become frightened of him.

Ask someone else, they'll show you a letter in which he's written: "As they say back in the city, grab ass, do cock."

So, the street. Clients perhaps. This and that. No *place*, though. Not a square inch. *Homeless*. Stupid word. Stupid country. Stupid world.

TEMPTATION

It was at the very moment that Plato overcame his sense of devious-
ness and betrayal and faithlessness and understood that if what
Socrates said was to be truly grasped by the multitudes to whom it
was ultimately meant to be addressed, it would have to be simplified,
schematized, and so distorted, but there was nothing for it.

At that moment, just after dawn, before the haze of the wood
cooking fires of the city would have risen into the crystalline light
of an early-summer Athenian day, at that very moment, not terribly
far away in the vast sense of distance he already inhabited, the Bud-
dha felt the axle of the earth and the overflowing crown of the fir-
mament shudder, so that he had to put his hand on the earth to
comfort her, to hold everything together, understanding even as his
palm touched the moist, cool, tremulous granules of soil that this,
someday, in half the minds of the world and half the reaches of the
galaxies, would be known forever as his temptation.

CLEAVAGE

Scanning left to right, right to left, then down in, deep in, and once again, left, right, in, the woman at the dinner party with a truly extraordinary bosom checks how things are down there, and things are fine down there, the men all think, trying not to stare, it's hunky-dory there, until she looks once perhaps too often, or maybe too self-consciously or too admiringly, then something changes, alters, just a bit . . .

A silent sigh—a loosening of breath, attention, tension—runs rapidly around the table because men and mates now, as though a truce had been effected, realize this isn't just finery on display here, exotic or erotic, but something rather in the realm of commerce and exchange: assets are being estimated, instruments of wealth and worth.

BIRD

What possibly could it be, that flash of not quite blood red but a more luminous Brueghel crimson, then a banner of Ghirlandaio sunflower yellow that whenever this morning I hear a bird cry in the yard and go to the window darts off before I can tell anything more than that it's been there, leaving me straining my eyes and trying to imagine what possible evolutionary choices could arrive at such a double seductive triumph of color, like two jets of paint on a palette, and why.

PHOBIA

So she'd missed another trip, had let him make the plans, then had canceled, canceled again, so what? They're barely speaking anyway, as usual, let him go himself, he'd have a better time without her anyway.

But that's not why she stayed home, and neither was it fear. Traveling itself didn't make her afraid, she could deal with anxiety, lord knows. It was rather that if she went with him, she wouldn't be where she should be, *here*, because if she weren't *here*, the change she'd waited all these years, these decades for, that alteration of existence which wouldn't merely dispel her fears, but, more important, would bring the ultimate but so far unachieved fullness she knew her destiny held for her. All of that might, no, surely would, again elude her because the crucial change would arrive in the space in which she normally existed, but she wouldn't *be* there.

And it would dissipate, be wasted, and when she came back from wherever she might have gone with him, if she'd gone with him, she'd remain the same as she'd always been, the very *same*, god, how much longer could she tolerate being who she'd so long been compelled to be with him? How risk the chance she'd awaited with such vigilance?

All these years of patience squandered, wasted.

No, stay here, mindful, watchful, dedicated, though staying here meant, yes, sacrifices, they would be redeemed in her newborn configuration.

How could he comprehend that, with his coarse, "Let's go, let's just go," and his unrelenting anger at her not?

HINGES

All the while the team of doctors, the anesthesiologist of which was my son-in-law, Michael Burns, were trying to find exactly where the sixteen-year-old boy who'd been shot and brought into their inner-city emergency room was bleeding, the boy kept trying to explain how it happened, how he'd ended up on this particular night of his short life shot, but they only cared *where*, the why to them was at least now of no moment—something had been severed, but because of all the oozing blood they couldn't figure out what.

All the time they were deciding they shouldn't put him to sleep until they found exactly what was happening inside him, all the time they were searching to find where the slug had entered, where it had come out, and what was torn, punctured or frayed, the boy kept explaining, explaining.

Michael, always the soul of calm, relives telling about it the sense of the doctors' frustration, the futility of their haste as the boy began to speak more slowly, his eyelids on their intricate hinges began to swing shut, opened again, the boy still trying to tell them, tell them, then shut once more, to stay.

So cunningly crafted they are, those hinges; so delicate those inch-wide sheets of matter, so nearly translucent seen from without, then so ruthlessly not.

A CERTAIN HALF HOUR IN BED

And after the moaning and groaning, the sobbing, the singing, the roaring, after all had subsided, you were given to understand that was that.

Not you, *that*.

GODS ETC

Perhaps occasionally we should feel compassion for our gods, even offer condolence for how they have to abide being armored in gold, dusted in gold, melted to molten gold, then fixed in gestures of might and tacked to the ribs of our temples, our prayers burning their eyes like soot . . .

How much by now must they desire not to lurk quavering in cerebellum or hypothetical soul, when all they may well have really wanted when they brought us forth were beings equipped with senses to share their delight in creation, to marvel with them before trees, seas, mountains, to say "Look!" with them, "Look!"

And that might be why they made us so fatally curious, why we trekked through savanna and valley—what's out there? what will be next?—our noses twitching like rabbits', our ears perked like hounds'.

And what of the gods who were boiled up after we'd already arrived on the scene? Is it as strange for them as for us that Jesus lived barely the distance from here to Detroit from Ovid or crazy Catullus—what, my goodness, would Jesus have thought of Catullus?—and that actual gods and their prophets arrived when we were already stomping around in our historical fun house? That Muhammad soared on his jet-propelled steed just as English was getting traction, Beowulf was hacking at Grendel, and Chaucer was already out there in sight?

But let's not leave out what at least seem to be the good-guy religions, Buddhism, Taoism, Bahá'í, because otherwise all we'd have are those with saints and martyrs ready to undergo suffering, to kill and be killed, the nuns with their breasts hacked off, or that horrid image in Bruges I'll never get out of my mind of a poor man screaming in the hideous silence of paint as he's dissected alive like a frog.

It can all be depressing—maybe we should go back and do some corrections the way we used to in school, where if you filled in the blank wrong you could erase. Maybe that's what we need now, to take the edge of a bone and scrape clean the parchment. It won't matter, though, will it? The words can go, but the gods will stay; the tunes go, the babble stays.

And we'll end up with black eraser crumbs in the arcs of our nails.

MONEY

He's thinking of the stock market, of the small amount of money he has invested. He's wondering whether the person at his bank who overlooks his investments is doing a good job. Then he thinks of the other, many times larger bank where he has his checking account, and wonders whether there would be someone there who might be better at finding ways for his money to earn more money. This would seem reasonable, since, the bank being larger, there would be a greater possibility of someone working in it being more perspicacious and daring.

Then he's taken all at once with an image of the absurdity of all those souls, those dedicated, passionate, often brilliant souls spending all their time day and night trying to outsmart one another in the unending contest of growing money. "How money multiplies ..." Rilke puts it, "naked, right there on stage ... guaranteed to increase your potency ..."

So many of them, he thinks, trying to annul each other's monetary decisions, their actions, their lives, really, given the fervor with which they attend to these matters. Then he has a vision of the entire planet filled, charged, clogged with the people who manipulate money. Enormous the world, he thinks, and he quails, he feels himself actually quail before the notion of the multitudes of money people, and beyond them the even more limitless multitudes of human beings on earth whose well-being, or actual existence, depends on those others. And he feels, he really does feel the planet faltering under the weight of so many lives, each laden with its vision of dollars and euros and rupees and rubles, and he can sense the earth tipping, as though it could tip, and falling, not like a planet falling from its usual orbit, but falling rather like a piece of pottery onto the floor and shattering.

Too many, too much, he finds himself thinking, though he knows how ridiculous he's being, how childish, he can't help it: Too many, too much.

But still, how not admire them, the dollar folk who make money reproduce? The way they must be able to cleverly fan out stock certificates or actual currency as magicians do cards; the way sometimes they must toss everything up in the air over their desks and sit back to see where it will all come down, or if it will.

Sometimes perhaps it must simply stay up there, like a spaceship, or an impalpable umbrella covering the earth, the earth of un-money-moving mortals, who, shuddering here in the shadows, can perceive nothing, do nothing but tremble in anxiety and awe while we wait to see which money calamity, which pulverization will take us next, which sense of being swept away in wild gales of want.

FRIENDSHIP

Some days the best thing in a museum isn't the art, the paintings or statues, even those, say, from ancient Greece—a frieze of women, their dresses pouring like water—but maybe because you're depressed, or distracted, or too something anyway to be anything but hopeless about human aspiration and hope, it's rather the people who are there with you, the schoolchildren earnestly measuring and sketching, the young couple embracing—he loves her but she loves, you can tell, her new dress, as soon as he lets her go she runs her hands down the panels of its shining fabric again—even the woman who talks too loudly to her husband in some indecipherable language and who when the guard tries to shush her beams brightly back at him as though he'd said something amusing, and the rather rough-looking guy who's obviously been dragged here by his wife, a plump, pleasant-looking woman. He plops down on a bench, loudly sighs, then makes believe he's collapsing of exhaustion, ending up horizontal, staring wide-eyed at the ceiling as though he were dead.

Right past him I notice a relief, Greek too, that I've never looked at closely. Two men with shields, their bodies at first apparently at ease, shaking hands; then I notice one is doing so a bit more insistently than the other, his hand more forcefully, rigidly extended. The other is merely allowing his hand to be taken—his slight tilt away and the slouch of his shoulders indicate reluctance, or suspicion—perhaps he's been offended and if this is an apology, he doesn't want to let his having been offended go, or not completely, not yet.

"His having been offended . . ." Peculiar to think so many centuries after.

The lazy husband and his wife are gone, so are the lovers. Just me, and the guard, defending those once-fleeting emotions in stone.

ANOTHER DISTURBING DEATH

At a conference I attended last week a young woman assisting the organizers introduced herself to me as I was checking in at the desk of the hotel, then moved towards me into a closeness I wasn't prepared for, so, face-to-face like that, I could feel a tiny, quite trivial but palpable erotic linkage set in resonance between us, though when I backed away a bit, to my relief it stopped.

She comes back to me when I think, think again of another young woman about whom I read in the *Times* this morning: the playwright Sarah Kane. It was in a more than merely admiring review of a play she'd written that opened last night in New York. The name was familiar, though at first only slightly. I read the rest of the article and in the second paragraph discovered that the playwright had committed suicide, hanging herself, at twenty-eight, and that since then her plays, including this one, had been great successes in London, and now in New York.

It was then that I thought I remembered her name: Sarah Kane. She'd written to me when my books first came out in the United Kingdom, a fan letter, but a little more familiar than most, smarter and better written, and so I wrote back, and we began a brief correspondence, sporadic on my part, more constant on hers. Her last letter came just as I was leaving for a reading in London, and in it she said that she'd come to the reading and we could finally meet.

I was pleased. I'd been curious about her, and I suppose there was an undercurrent of hoping she'd be attractive (in fantasy of course more than merely attractive), not because I had any yen for a sexual liaison—that wasn't in my repertoire of wishes for my life by then—but because—I'm loath to admit this but I'm a male and I suppose it's true—she'd be more interesting to talk to if she were beautiful.

When she came up to me at my reading and introduced herself, I was . . . well, disappointed is the only word for it. She was much younger than I'd thought she'd be, she looked to be twenty or so, and sported that kind of uniform depressed adolescents will employ that makes them look even more estranged than they might be: she wore combat boots, ill-fitting army-navy clothes, had kohl on her eyelids, black lipstick and nail polish, spiked dyed purple hair, and from her general expression appeared to be more than superficially troubled. To top it off, she was with a boy her own age who by how he slouched beside her looked to be going through the same sort of turmoil.

I'll say again that I hadn't been expecting anything of moment to happen between us, but still, I had been interested in her, if for no other reason because of the energy of the prose in her letters. Once we greeted each other, though, we didn't have much to say, and after an awkward interval she went off with her friend, or boyfriend, and I did whatever I was supposed to be doing.

I wish I could remember whether all this was before my reading, when it would have been more appropriate for me to move on to other things, or afterwards, when my turning from her could have seemed rude, and, to use a term I'd rather not, rejecting.

I never heard from her after that, and I doubt if she ever crossed my mind again, except perhaps as I was packing away that year's correspondence. Had she sent me poems? I can't remember: I know she wanted to write them, but don't know if she had, and now my papers are in their boxes and it would be all but impossible to find her letters.

She hanged herself, yet another one—there are so damned many, the sad beyond sad. The most recent was a young woman, Catherine's mother's goddaughter's daughter, twenty-one, whom I'd met only once when she was hardly more than a child, who hanged herself, too, and whose death shocked me profoundly, though I didn't quite know why: it just hit me, hard, and I found myself crying aloud.

At least Sarah Kane is famous now, like Sylvia Plath . . . If it really was Sarah Kane at all. Perhaps I'm misremembering entirely; maybe it was another girl, who never achieved notoriety, for whatever that would be worth.

Something odd: at that conference last week, during a conversation at lunch with the young woman I mentioned before and a few other people, for some reason the talk turned to suicide, and she confessed she often thought of it—even said that she was tempted by it. It was hard for me to take her seriously—she seemed quite cheerful, with a kind of frank openness in her manner that made the notion of her even thinking of killing herself absurd. I hope I was right.

Sarah Kane, though, or whoever it was, it's hard not to think again about our meeting. Did I, with a gesture so subtle I wouldn't have even known I gave it, establish that there was to be no real link between us? Would she have sensed it? As the woman last week, by moving such an infinitesimal distance closer to me, had established her if not erotic then let's say theatrical interest in me, had I, perhaps by barely moving my head, barely turning a bit askance to her, Sarah Kane or the other, let her know with a similar clarity that there would be no such drama between us, even of the most harmless sort?

But wait, her never getting in touch with me again, was that a rejection of sorts on her part as well? Had I disappointed her, her expectation of some connection to me, so that afterwards she'd have thrust me out of her ken? Cut me off and out?

It wouldn't matter, though, would it? I'm probably just trying to evade any possible feather of responsibility for what ultimately happened to her. The question should be whether there was some way I might have helped her.

Difficult to think all this. Forgive me, Sarah Kane. Or that unknown, unknowable girl: you, too, please forgive.

APOLLO OR DIONYSUS

Which?

   Quick! Which?

   Too late . . . Too late again.

FUR

I dreamed that my dead friend's wife, whom he had worshipped and warred with their entire marriage, was berating him: "Sex!" she was sobbing, frenzied, "my sexual despair—you should have known."

Then my friend, apparently chastened in my dream by a tempest of such resentment and rage, assumed the body of a massive animal, imposing but vulnerable, with no fangs, talons, or claws, and assured her he would no longer journey to heaven, the way was too arduous, the distance too great.

He preferred, he diffidently murmured, to remain where he was, the implication being in hell, the implication being further that something beyond had agreed with her conviction of injustice and had inflicted a punishment upon him in the form of this shocking, bestial transformation.

He gave no indication of suffering, though, nor did he turn from his wife in shame or chagrin. It seemed not to matter to him that this was a dream: his gaze was steady, his new fur shone.

CATTLE

In a pasture a herd of cows, one of which has her head between the strands of the barbed-wire fence so she can reach what she must consider some especially succulent mouthfuls of grass. Her thick neck pushes up against the wire, lifting it: she has to feel the barbs digging at her, trying to tear her skin, her flesh, but she's unconcerned. It's almost noon; in a little while, as they do every day at this hour, all the cattle will stop grazing and lie down. They don't sleep, but rather just lie there, seeming to need to rest from the exertion of existing.

MEDITATION

The dancer at the dinner party, sitting on the floor, plate beside her, neck high, breasts high, spine impossibly straight, legs curled beneath her in the lotus, her whole carriage informed with an insistent but gentle tension, drifts away into herself, regards her feet, runs her hand across them, one at a time, instep first, then outer edge, then across, over the muscular ball, polished smooth but unbunioned, like a child's . . .

Now she flexes the toes of her left foot, tilting her head towards them, critically attentive to their workings; then tenses both feet, hard, once, then three, four short, sharp but still light pullings followed by a general relaxation.

Then the other foot, same ritual, meticulous, same deep, pure, intellectually rigorous absorption . . .

Then she surfaces abruptly, is back among us, smiling, chatting, never having lost the thread, her feet beneath her now, though something utterly forbidden to the rest of us, utterly unknown.

SCHULZ

Bruno Schulz, the great writer and artist, the story of his death, the myth it might well be, so much hyperbole, frank untruths left over from that time—it seems our human curse to have to exaggerate to make the worst things even worse so we can more appropriately lift ourselves from our lethargies to respond to them.

Schulz, under the protection of an SS man, or a Gestapo chieftain, someone anyway who was watching out for him because Schulz was painting murals for the nursery of the Nazi monster's child, cheerful paintings that have been pried from their wall now and spirited away to the Holocaust museum in Jerusalem . . .

Schulz was shot to death by another German officer—am I repeating something everyone knows?—who it's said was piqued because Schultz's Nazi had shot *his* Jew, his dentist it was, and for the sake of vengeance, or who knows perhaps for some other reason entirely, some petty jealousy, even some love thing, shot the other shooter's Jew, who was Schulz, the inimitable, immortal Schulz.

"You shoot my Jew, I shoot yours." One vermin for another, and how horrible, more than that, how insane to contemplate that Schulz, as Jew, had become a kind of *currency*, a medium of exchange, and that the other, nameless, vanished Jew, the one who's lost to us in every way, no image, no story, one of that unthinkable infinitude, becomes in history something like a slug, a false coin, a chunk of worthless lead to slide in a slot.

MARCH

The last gasp of winter: on one neighbor's patio one last infinitesimal Antarctica of ice amid their children's discarded, soiled summer toys. No wind; the branch of the locust tree beyond the window hasn't moved it seems for a century as it waits for the thaw.

Everything else waits, too, except for the squirrels who come to attack the armored bird feeder, shaking it, gnawing and clawing it, to no avail. A solitary cardinal waits nearby for them to give up so it can eat breakfast.

Our other, poorer neighbor's white butane tank, stripped of the weeds that in summer obscure it, glares in the sunlight, raw, unseemly, like a breast inappropriately unclothed in the painful chill.

SYBIL

What must I do, to her, to myself, to believe or imagine I can believe in her? Ocher hills, I think, pale, dusty low green shrubs of wild thyme; darker cypresses, "cemetery trees" they're called these days; then squat clay or stacked stone houses, a cave, a crypt, with off to the side a priest or suppliant asleep on the still blood-soaked skin of a slaughtered sheep or goat.

Then I see, across a hillside, something moving, taking up some small portion of my field of vision—does my anticipation make it seem to take up more? When my eyes focus on it, yes, perhaps, but when I look away, it seems precisely what it should be, in scale and density. Is it she? How know?

What's more apprehensible is what I smell: a stink, a stench, like something I sniffed once in an unswept, unwatered cage of starving bears; or in the plastic container I opened by mistake with months-old chunks of seething rotted meat inside it: the way my head snapped back without my meaning it to. All that, mingled with never-washed secret female flesh; soured menstrual emissions, rotted teeth, scab and self-inflicted filth.

And what could she possibly look like? I'm stuck with such trite imagery—madwoman from a play, wild woman from a film; disheveled mane, rags of burlap, feet and ankles bound in tattering strips like compresses on running wounds.

And then she speaks: whispered hiccupings of disconnected consonants, like someone choking on food, someone else's throat funneled down by illness. And what she finally says: the cadence is wrong, the lilt, the violence of voice with which she's afflicted won't allow for de-encrypting.

No language music—I know enough to know there'd be none of that: a grunt instead, a cry of rage.

Do I yet believe in her? Do I remember why I came to her, and what I meant to ask? What I meant to know?

PLASTIC

Stripping the annoyingly tough vacuum seal from the showerhead I'm trying to install, I find that instead of chrome, it's plated plastic, a tab of it already peeled away, exposing the dull white poly-something beneath.

Later, on a stroll through the dusk, passing the graveyard in our town, the plastic comes to mind and, abruptly with it, I'll never quite understand why, the image of the dead in their ancient coffins beneath us in the earth.

I'll never know either why their fists are clenched, their jaws are clenched, eyes wide in either terror or rage—I can't tell. They're strung on themselves in a hideous, unrelenting tension, like demented wires on a harp.

It had been such a serenely softening evening. The blushing clouds in the west, new flowers flashing, starlings, fields flowing away into the distance—you know: the distance, the sweet, undevouring distance; then this.

GOETHE

As she drank from a tin cup on the sloped wooden lid of a well, she slipped on a streak of damp, lost her footing, and tumbled, if not quite head over heels then almost—her long, smooth legs a klutzy tangle, her shapely arms stupidly, futilely flailing before she landed, hard, on her admirably shapely backside and sat there in tears.

Pig that I was, the image of her falling hooked into my psyche and dug achingly in like a thorn—I couldn't force myself to release the image of her clumsy bungling.

She had no idea from whence after came my coolness, my coldness, and how could I admit to her I was so shallow that one single instance of non-beauty could so exacerbate my fear of it?

"Much can be made from the ugly," wrote Goethe, "from beauty not a thing."

MEETINGS

In the part of my mind that's not unlike a second-rate hotel in a medium-sized university city—cheap carpets, sham crystal chandeliers—the theorists are holding their annual or so convention. Even before the outset, so much anticipation, so much of a buzz! New concepts to be explicated, imprecise ideas set to right: smiles all around, warm greetings of old competitors and friends.

As the sessions begin, the lobbies empty except for a few deconstructionists plotting their tactics and some already forlorn-looking language poets hawking books that haven't sold for decades and won't ever. I wander into a meeting and soon realize everything I know is obsolete, out of date, passé—Freud, the unconscious, id—all, I discover to my chagrin, are threatened with no longer existing. And Marxian dialectic? Don't be absurd … Even Lévi-Strauss's bricolage …

"Stop!" I want to protest. "I need them," but no one's listening—the discussion has turned to mind and brain—qualia, whatever they might be—do I have them?—and then somehow from that to moral relativism: "When we aver," a forceful voice demands from the stage, "it is virtuous to tell the truth, what are we saying?" Yes, I think, just what?

Something like headache takes me now. Headache? Isn't theory supposed to make you feel better? I drift from session to session—I'm not educated for this; too many hours squandered in daydreams and half-realized verse.

At last, adjournment: the room taken by the frenzy of chairs knocked from their rational rows; the deliberations I thought crucial to my peace of mind have come to naught; I hardly recall them. Out the revolving door to the street, I wait for a bus to take me to wherever I should be next. Maybe an opera or a ball game or a pet store where they'll let me play with the puppies?

Or might one fancy a grander venue, gilt lobbies, politicos, the elegant rich, even film stars? . . .

Hey, there's Gwyneth Paltrow! Gwyneth, over here! . . . I think she's looking at me! . . .

No, she's not.

LATE

If you're not careful, of an evening, after dinner, still at table, late, having eaten well and drunk perhaps too well, drifting through the chat, the dog beside you sated with its table scraps yet gazing up at you with that plaintive, ever-avid wish to please which is its destiny, if you're not careful, you might glance over at the photo on the mantel of the person who's been gone already all these many years, and she, smiling shyly at whoever trapped the slice of light that so thoroughly contains her, will have something in her eyes like longing, want, something saying, *Let me be more vivid in you, please, be in firmer union with you, otherwise the life I almost have again within you might not be complete, but like the dog's might always lack, always need, not your pity, but something you can't give, which lasts as long, and burns as much.*

FORCE

At the medieval festival in the town below the Château Gaillard, the fortified castle on a cliff over the Seine that William the Conqueror caused to be constructed in the eleventh century, a small boy, by the sheer force of his unreasonable, intimidating insistence and persistence, has cowed his larger older brother into letting him appropriate the plastic battle-ax their parents had bought the brother.

The weapon is one of those remarkable reproductions manufactured these days, probably in China; it looks exactly like the weapons the war-mad Norman invaders wielded to brain the hapless peasants who had the misfortune to dwell along the river and the temerity to try to protect their farmsteads from those ruthless pillagers.

The younger brother soon tires of the thing and drops it on the lawn, where it falls onto a clump of tiny yellow flowerets so bright they look lacquered, one of which is just now bending under the weight of a wasp of a duller, ambiguous yellow, and I imagine that if the child should venture near, it might well for no particular reason sting him, as one of his ilk stung me yesterday when all I'd done was place my hand on the table beside it to lift my glass of wine.

PROTESILAUS

Such a depressing story, about the first Greek warrior to land at Troy, who was also the first to die in the mad battles there, and his wife, Laodamia, whose raving grief for her husband so moved the gods that they allowed him to return to her, but only for a limited time. When they dragged him back again to the realm of the dead, she killed herself.

The saddest part of it is that there's nothing there to make a real tragedy, it's just a tale. The drama of Alcestis, who sacrificed her life for her husband's, and Hecuba, who Dante recounts was driven mad by sorrow, barking like a dog, were intricate blendings of necessity and pride and love. Laodamia's was merely an example of a woman's devotion, or it could be read as her inability to extricate herself from attachment to another mortal.

There might have been a more dramatic ending, though. How, when he, Protesilaus, the husband, was brought back to life, he believed that he was there to stay, that the iron force of his wife's passion for him had outdone death: so tremulously grateful he must have been to her.

But when they reeled him back down again to Hades, might he have blamed the imperfection of that same passion? Perhaps he remembered how easily distracted she could be, and how sometimes when he pulled her to him she'd whine, "You're hurting me."

How could such a simpleminded creature have done this to him, let them take him from her? "*Again*," he may have snarled as she faded from his sight, "*you let your passion fail again.*"

THE INFANTICIDE

A great space in my skull, she says. When she stops crying. Before she starts crying again. *A space.*

She means *mind*. Space in her mind. Wherein the responsibility for her act, of murder, the prosecutor at her trial says, is contained.

I see flashes, she says. She means *in flashes*. She means, as in a storm. *I see her*, she means her child, *and she's crying and then nothing then I see her in her bath and she's smiling. Then nothing again.*

The car she and the child were riding in until she stopped by the edge of the lake and got out.

"The baby had made progress," testifies an accusing neighbor, *"she'd almost started to walk."*

"I've never seen anyone so depressed," the court psychologist avers. *"She's a nurse. She knew what was coming. She knew what 'degenerative' means, what 'hopeless.' She'd seen it before she had to live it."*

Another woman with a child with the same affliction: *"None of you know. You can't know. A mother gives life, can't she take it away? I think of doing it, too, but I turn myself to stone and I don't."*

In my skull, says the one not turned to stone. *In my storm. That storm in my skull. The water rose. I found myself on the shore. Then the space in my skull.*

She means *mind*. She means *mind in my mind*.

OLD

Strung up how many lifetimes ago between the back porch of a derelict house and the dilapidated toolshed out behind, an old-fashioned, all but decomposed sash-cord clothesline is caught up in the bitter autumn evening wind. Drawn tight like a bow or lyre string, it's released, only to slacken impotently, sway helplessly for a long moment, and be taken up again, stretched and shaken tremulously along its weary length.

Too worn out by its seasons to sound again, it still perhaps dreams of singing, dreams its softened strands firm again, the songs it can barely remember howling out into the roar.

A BEDROOM IN AFRICA

The bedroom is Agatha's, and Agatha is our ward, our "niece," she calls herself, something like our stepdaughter. Every month we send some money—our "precious money," wrote Elizabeth Bishop when she lived in Brazil—to help her grow up, be educated, survive, and we hope one day have a life she can love. Her bedroom is on the outskirts of Kampala, Uganda, which is on the outskirts of the world but which to itself is the very center of the world and of the universe.

Stand on a corner, and you'll see. As in the universe, everything rushes away from everything else, or towards it. Except the human beings. Most human beings not in vehicles in Kampala look to be standing still. They're waiting, on corners, in front of buildings, many of which are waiting also, to be completed, to have their half-erected walls made taller, their blank windows filled with frames and glass. The human beings wait more patiently than that of course, in doorways, on curbs, on the dusty sidewalks. They wait for it's never quite clear what. For galaxies to evolve, universes to start over—a saner Big Bang this time, which will give them something, occupations, pastimes, things to do besides wait, things to do to no longer be wretchedly poor, no longer starve, kill one another, die of war, die of AIDS.

Yet while so many are waiting, the entire center of the city is dense with traffic, endless herds of cars, buses, trucks, motorbikes, all spewing stinking, suffocating fumes. Everything of importance seems related in one way or another to the combustion engine. A constant sense of hurry, swoop, stall: people mount motorcycles, ride a few yards, get off, get into buses, jump out; trucks growl and grind their gears; cars end up face-to-face at intersections, honking like furious geese; people dodge in and out of the incessant stream of vehicles, but it's the vehicles, the trucks and buses and anything else with an engine that maintain their dominion. Between the people who are waiting and the traffic that refuses to, the whole society seems in a state of explosion, with so little order that it's hard to believe anything can be accomplished.

Agatha's bedroom, though, is in a quiet place some miles out at the edge of the city. It's forty or fifty feet long, about twenty feet wide; four windows in the back wall, two on each side, three and a door in the front. The walls were probably white not long ago but are now a weary half gray. Their tint isn't unpleasant, though, and the bedroom is very clean, not a crumb on the floor, not a glimmer of dust. The path to it through the grounds of the school is neatly swept, too. Students stroll or hurry along them, some sit at desks in the classroom buildings, which have openings for windows but no frames or glass.

Agatha loves and is proud of her bedroom, she badly wanted us to see it. In it are three rows of double-decker beds, with about three feet between them; ten bunks in each row, so Agatha has fifty-nine roommates, fifty-nine siblings, I suppose you could say, since all are orphans, their parents deceased of civil war or AIDS or ... We're not informed of all the possibilities.

The ceiling of the room is quite high, and most of the beds have above them a dress on a hanger suspended from the ceiling by a cord: they remind me of the pulley systems factory workers in our own country once used to hang their street clothes in the rooms where they changed into and back out of the overalls they wore while they worked. When they worked. Remember when men worked? Remember the time before we all seemed, like galaxies, to be rushing away from one another out of the cosmos of work?

Under each bed is a plastic basin; on top of some lie small suitcases of stiffened paper, imitations of the luggage young people used before backpacks became ubiquitous. When the girls get into bed, the suitcases will have to go somewhere else, underneath, I suppose, with the basins. There are no extra shoes under the beds: the girls must possess only the pair they're wearing.

Agatha has a suitcase, which means she has someone to visit: we know who—a grandmother, just one—no one else. A poor grandma who has lived long enough to see all her children die before her, one after another. In her photo Grandma has deep lines in her face— "dark ravines," César Vallejo wrote of the consequence of life's blows.

Agatha is very tall and very slim, with narrow feet and the short, clipped hair that everyone, men and women, has in Uganda. Although we've been exchanging letters for some years, we meet for the first time in person at a lunch arranged by a pleasant, lively woman from the agency that manages our contributions. Agatha at first was very quiet, though in her semiannual letters she expresses frank affection for her Auntie and Uncle—Auntie Catherine especially she's close to in the letters. After a while she relaxed—she's seventeen, it's hard anyway to calm down at that age, but she relaxed or relented, who would know just from what, and chatted, mostly with Catherine. Meanwhile, I sat quietly as the world beyond still stretched away from us, out and away into the universe.

I realized during our meal that whenever I looked across at Agatha she was already gazing at me, not shyly, not furtively, but with a somber, reflective expression. She seemed to be examining me, as though I presented a puzzle to her, a mystery to solve. Gravitation perhaps; the equations of gravity-energy-mass.

When Agatha watched me that way, I had no idea how to respond, what expression I was supposed to assume. Two things came to my mind: Agatha has had more profound life experience in her seventeen years, has been exposed to more suffering than I have in my many decades. And the other is that she's probably never used or perhaps even heard the word "suffering." Or not outside of prayer service, where it wouldn't mean the same thing.

Most likely, I thought, the way she regarded me might have something to do with me as a kind of substitute father. Had she ever known her real father? I don't think so, but how ask a question like that? Anyway, was she trying to find an emotion in herself that would be something like what people feel, she must believe, when they gaze across a table at their father? I don't remember either of my children ever looking at me with that degree of seriousness. Did I ever look at my father that way, except in my mind? I suppose in my mind.

When it's time to say goodbye, Agatha and Catherine will embrace, kiss each other's cheeks, but when Agatha and I come together the ritual of embrace will suddenly be very complicated, we won't manage it properly: her head will turn at the wrong moment, or mine will; I'll move towards her too quickly and my lips will collide with the side of her forehead, then bump into her eyebrow—such an elaborate procedure.

At another orphanage we're taken to visit, for smaller children, where Agatha used to be in residence, it was lunchtime and porridge was being ladled out: pale, and blank, unadorned with anything but itself. The oatmeal of my childhood, even when we were "poor," when our mother was fretting so because of our being poor, was speckled with honey or sugar. And I still could barely abide its blandness.

It's always been unclear and worrisome to me how our food reaches us. Getting anything, an apple, say, from its tree off in the country somewhere, over the distance between there and here, to and through a market, to and through the store. According to what I've read, most poor Africans, meaning I gather most Africans, live on one meal a day, and sometimes not even that. I can hardly conceive how even in prosperous societies so many millions of people are fed, and sufficiently nourished, or nearly, with so little to-do, but here in Africa the to-do is blatantly evident: the civic atmosphere is so thick, so dense, it feels like everything, produce, food, clothes, anything, has to be dragged through it—the very ground, the air, the roads, seem to resist. When food does arrive somewhere, it must be a rare treasure. The women in markets stack their ten or twenty tomatoes in ingenious and precarious pyramids and crouch reverently behind them.

New Jersey, where I grew up, used to be a mostly agricultural state. "Truck farming," the business was called when we learned about it in grammar school, and in those days as soon as you left the cities and the then-sparse suburbs, there were fields of potatoes, tomatoes, corn; even pastures with grazing cows. That's all but gone now, there are only "garden apartments" and endless tracts of modest houses, and lately of ungainly "McMansions" sprawled across the once productive land. There are still a few farms in corners of the state, but with the ever-exploding price of real estate, the farmers can't make enough by farming to match what they would by selling their land, and when you do happen to pass a farm, it feels like an exercise in nostalgia.

My father-in-law told me that in Paris during the second war there was so little food that the gardens of the Louvre were planted with potatoes. During those same years in America there were "victory gardens"—people with even small yards were encouraged to grow vegetables. We lived in a flat with a concrete slab driveway behind it, but my parents had some friends around the corner with a house and a yard, and they spent many evenings and weekends companionably working in their garden. The strangest thing, though: we went away on a trip, just for a week to see our relatives in

Rochester, and when we came back the people had sold the house and disappeared, so we never ate a mouthful of the food my parents had worked so hard to cultivate.

We didn't go hungry, then or ever, but so many images from that time still haunt me: starved bodies in concentration camps and, no less harrowing, children begging for scraps and dying of hunger in the doomed ghettos of Eastern Europe, then after the war people in bombed-out cities waiting in long lines for a bowl of soup. It all stays with me, and I keep wondering if there ever were a real crisis, if we had to grow our own food again, whether there'd be anyone left who'd know how to make those sterilized suburban lawns bring sustenance forth once more.

But back to Agatha, who is telling us now that she wants to become a nurse. That would be splendid. Wouldn't that truly be splendid? And she is so pleased that we like her bedroom. Some of her friends smile at us, too. They glow like the light from the windows, the light from the distant planet of earth where I thought I lived. The earth we once thought we owned.

After our visit with Agatha, we become tourists and travel out from Kampala, Uganda, out past the school of Agatha's bedroom, out past the highways where humans wait and wait, and through the highway town where a Muslim imam strolled in the brilliant white of his robe, as white as the white on the newborn goats in a yard beside the road. The buildings in the smaller towns almost all tilt, their walls out of plumb, to use a builder's term. What a meaningless phrase it is here, what an unreasonable demand the word asks of the structures people contrive to erect against the insistent demands of gravity. Things lean, they sag, they teeter, tip, and must shudder and rock in wind. The only real issue must be whether or not the hut, the market stall, the windowless, doorless church falls or doesn't fall, or at least doesn't fall too quickly, so that it can be propped up again, buttressed again with another sapling, another scrap of broken wood ... No wonder Agatha is proud of her bedroom. She's surely aware of how rare and precious are its upright walls, its solid cement floors, its hard, smooth plaster.

One morning in a game park we come upon some lions. All but one quickly slip away into the bush, but to that one, a female, it's as though we don't exist: she comes towards us with an expression of raging indifference, disdain, for us, for all humans, for galaxies and the cosmos. Her shoulders jutting and rolling, her jaw swinging loosely in defiant decontraction, she doesn't even deign to regard us, contemptuously sauntering by us, allowing us for her own amusement to exist for this single instant in the unfathomable golden substance of her thought.

SIXTY

When I offhandedly remarked to my father how sad it was that his good friend Sol would be dying next year he startled and asked what do you mean and I answered well he'll be sixty won't he so he'll die and my father said what are you talking about and I said well when you're sixty that's when you die everybody knows that and then my father "disabused" me—is that the term?—of that notion which it turns out was true for the men on the island—Kea—where the poet Simonides came from because when they hit sixty all the males drank hemlock and removed themselves got out of the way you might put it which doesn't seem like that bad an idea when I wake creaking and crackling and drag myself out of my sleep and also sometimes just seeing something like that half-fossilized woman yesterday in the street old old with a too-short skirt—"mini" are they still called?—bright tights high leather boots thick makeup head shaved and one long earring dangling and my god what's she thinking I thought then glimpsed in my mind what pleasure for her it must have been to put her face on choose the outfit unroll the tights don the sweater hook on the earring then *hup* out the door and I remembered also what it was for myself this morning when I was shaving number sixty long gone old yellow teeth like teeth in a skull then

I saw in the glass indeed a skull my skull orbs dead as moons cracked grin leering and how could I have let myself get so old I thought I must not have paid enough attention I must have left too many days only partly put to use otherwise it would have taken longer to get here longer so much longer

AGAIN

One of my grandsons is running through the park towards me to show me something he's found—a long white feather—I can see it from here—probably from one of the herons that come at dawn to fish in the pond.

It doesn't matter which grandson it is: in my memory, it could be one, or another, or all—I'd prefer it were all, each in his brilliant singularity, each in his union with the rest.

There's a broad plane tree between us, and for some reason my grandson as he runs keeps moving left and then right, so he disappears behind the trunk of the tree, appears again, disappears, appears, vivid in the brilliant sunlight, again is gone, again is there, all the while beaming with pride at bearing such treasure to share with me.

Also he calls my name each time he appears, and as I stand waiting, listening, watching him materialize again, it comes to me that if that old legend of having your life flash before you as you die is true, I'll have this all again, and again.

ACKNOWLEDGMENTS

ACKNOWLEDGMENTS

"Books, Damned Books" was originally
published in *Poem* (London, 2013).

"Catherine's Laughter" was originally published as a
chapbook by Sarabande Press (Louisville, Kentucky, 2013).

"Scents" was originally published in
Tin House (Portland, Oregon, 2014).

The following poems were originally published in
a limited-edition book, *Sixty*, by David Sellers at Pied
Oxen Printers (Hopewell, New Jersey, 2014): "Bird,"
"The Broom," "Carts," "Hinges," "The Infanticide,"
"A Jew, a Road, Some Crows," "Listening," "Math,"
"Old," "Plastic," "Sixty," and "They Call This."